PILGRIM'S PATH

A STUDY OF THE PSALMS

ELIZABETH HEAD BLACK

Pilgrim's Path: A Study of the Psalms
© 2021 Elizabeth Head Black
All rights reserved.
Published in Houston, Texas by Bible Study Media, Inc.

ISBN # 978-1-942243-54-0
Ebook ISBN # 978-1-942243-55-7
Library of Congress Control Number: 2021923731

No part of this publication may be reproduced, stored in retrieval system, or transmitted in any form or by any means electronic, mechanical, photocopy, recording, or otherwise except for brief quotations in printed reviews, without the prior written permission of the publisher.
www.biblestudymedia.com.

Unless otherwise indicated, all Scripture quotations are from the ESV® Bible (The Holy Bible, English Standard Version®), copyright © 2001 by Crossway, a publishing ministry of Good News Publishers. Used by permission. All rights reserved.

Scripture quotations marked NIV are taken from the Holy Bible, New International Version®, NIV®. Copyright © 1973, 1978, 1984, 2011 by Biblica, Inc.™ Used by permission of Zondervan. All rights reserved worldwide. www.zondervan.com The "NIV" and "New International Version" are trademarks registered in the United States Patent and Trademark Office by Biblica, Inc.™

Scripture quotations marked KJV are from The Authorized (King James) Version. Rights in the Authorized Version in the United Kingdom are vested in the Crown. Reproduced by permission of the Crown's patentee, Cambridge University Press.

Scripture quotations marked MSG are taken from THE MESSAGE, copyright © 1993, 2002, 2018 by Eugene H. Peterson. Used by permission of NavPress, represented by Tyndale House Publishers. All rights reserved.

Printed in the United States of America.

*For my sons,
Milton and Nelson,
and in loving memory of my father,
William Burres Head III
who encouraged me to write a book about joy.*

FOR THE GLORY OF GOD!

TABLE OF CONTENTS

WELCOME	6
INTRODUCTION	8
DAILY DEVOTIONS	10

WEEK 1 - Creation Psalms — 12
Day 1: Psalm 19 — 16
Day 2: Psalm 104:1–18 — 19
Day 3: Psalm 104:19–35 — 21
Day 4: Psalm 145 — 24
Day 5: Psalm 29 — 26
Day 6: Psalm 33 — 28
Day 7: Psalm 33 — 30

WEEK 2 - Torah, Wisdom, and Well-Being Psalms — 34
Day 8: Psalm 119:1–89 — 38
Day 9: Psalm 119:90–176 — 41
Day 10: Psalm 1 — 43
Day 11: Psalm 112 — 46
Day 12: Psalm 14 — 49
Day 13: Psalm 15 — 52
Day 14: Psalms 131 and 133 — 55

WEEK 3 - Psalms of Lament — 58
Day 15: Psalm 13 — 62
Day 16: Psalm 86 — 64
Day 17: Psalm 41 — 67
Day 18: Psalm 74 — 70
Day 19: Psalm 109 — 73
Day 20: Psalm 88 — 75
Day 21: Psalm 50 — 78

WEEK 4 – Psalms of Internal Lament — 82
Day 22: Psalm 49 — 86
Day 23: Psalm 143 — 88
Day 24: Psalm 51 (Part 1) — 91
Day 25: Psalm 38 — 94
Day 26: Psalm 51 (Part 2) — 97
Day 27: Psalm 25 — 100
Day 28: Psalm 130 — 103

WEEK 5 - Psalms of Reorientation, Thanksgiving, and Enthronement	106
Day 29: Psalm 90	110
Day 30: Psalm 73	112
Day 31: Psalm 30	115
Day 32: Psalm 138	118
Day 33: Psalm 34	120
Day 34: Psalm 96	123
Day 35: Psalm 99	126

WEEK 6 - Psalms of Satisfaction, Confidence, and Praise	130
Day 36: Psalm 91	134
Day 37: Psalm 27	137
Day 38: Psalm 23	139
Day 39: Psalm 117	142
Day 40: Psalm 103	144
Day 41: Psalm 100	146
Day 42: Psalm 148	148

Study Guide

Using this Study	152
Outline of Each Session	154
Session 1: The Son of Man – Psalm 8	156
Session 2: The King of Glory – Psalm 24	162
Session 3: Threads of Faith – Psalm 137	168
Session 4: Gracious Forgiveness – Psalm 32	174
Session 5: Thy Kingdom Come – Psalm 98	180
Session 6: Unending Praise – Psalm 150	186
End Notes	192
APPENDICES	194
FREQUENTLY ASKED QUESTIONS	196
CIRCLES OF LIFE	198
SMALL GROUP COVENANT	199
SMALL GROUP CALENDAR	200
PRAYER & PRAISE JOURNAL	202
SMALL GROUP ROSTER	203
SMALL GROUP LEADER HELPS	204
LEADING FOR THE FIRST TIME	205
LEADERSHIP TRAINING 101	206
ACKNOWLEDGMENTS	209

Welcome

"Show me your ways, Lord, teach me your paths. Guide me in your truth and teach me, for you are God my Savior, and my hope is in you all day long."

PSALM 25:4–5, NIV

The Book of Psalms is a beautiful composition of poetry, ancient songs, and prayers that formed the Hebrew prayer book and hymnal that Jesus knew by heart. It has always drawn God's people to worship, leading them into a vibrant relationship with the living Lord. The Book of Psalms is also a book of wisdom, which uniquely prepares us for any spiritual, social, and emotional condition we can encounter in this life. To read the Psalms is to be given a powerful tool to walk through this circuitous and sometimes dangerous life with confidence, trust, and hope in the God who has prepared the way.

I am so pleased to announce this new study, *Pilgrim's Path: A Study of the Psalms*. It comes out of my lifelong affection for these Scriptures. For almost thirty years, I have connected with the Psalms by reading them daily, allowing them to shape my prayer life, and consequently my whole spiritual walk. The Book of Psalms has been a "matchless primer"[1] of theological instruction and practical wisdom, a guide to authentic prayer, a model for true worship, and a healing balm for my soul. The Psalms have been a mainstay for my faith. My prayer is that they will be the same for you.

My love for these verses has manifested itself in my ministry over the years. I have taught several studies on the Psalms, exploring the many ways they comfort and strengthen us emotionally and spiritually. I published a devotional book, *Hand in Hand: Walking with the Psalms through Loneliness* (Radiant Star Books, 2014), that highlights the irrefutable presence of God in our lives. This study, however, addresses the powerful Scriptures through a more theological lens. In that effort, I have devoted myself to the study of a wide array of theological resources on the Psalms, including books and commentaries by C. S. Lewis, John Stott, Dietrich Bonhoeffer, Eugene Peterson, Timothy Keller, Walter Brueggemann, and more.

Pilgrim's Path: A Study of the Psalms traces the magnificent, creative outreach of God to his people, maps out our response to him, identifies and guides us through the difficult struggles, and leads us back into his arms. In effect, we will walk a pilgrim's path, growing in our knowledge of God's character, discerning his will and purpose for our lives, learning to trust in him in every circumstance, and finding joy in his presence. More importantly, this study is designed to deepen our union with God through his Son Jesus Christ. *Pilgrim's Path: A Study of the Psalms* is for those who seek to know and love God more, to discover God's purpose for their lives, and to find life in it. Welcome to the journey.

Introduction

A Brief Introduction to the Psalms

The Book of Psalms is an ancient compilation of 150 poems, which are also lyrics to hymns, which are prayers at their core. For over 3,000 years[2], this inspired collection has formed the main prayerbook and hymnal for both the Jewish and Christian faiths and has been sung and prayed as an integral part of both private and public worship. The original Hebrew collection was referred to as "songs of praise." The subsequent Greek translation was *psalmoi*, which rendered the translation "psalms" in English. Eugene Peterson wrote that "all prayer pursued far enough, becomes praise."[3] *Pilgrim's Path: A Study of the Psalms* underscores this precept: when understood as a whole, they lead one to praise. May this be our joyful goal.

The Language of the Psalms

John Stott said that the Psalms "speak the universal language of the human soul."[4] They speak a language we know by heart. That is, in part, because they are poetic in nature. And yet, when we read them, we discover something new, something deeper, more meaningful, vibrant, and real. That is the imprint of the Holy Spirit, who is the primary author of these Scriptures. Therefore, the Psalms also speak a language of prayer and worship. They effectively lead us into an intimate dialogue with God. The Psalms are the verses *God teaches us* to pray to him, to sing to him. Because in God's presence we are compelled to "walk the talk," our conversation becomes our walk. In it, we find the Lord Jesus Christ guiding our footsteps, leading us in paths of wisdom and virtue, showing us new landscapes of freedom, beauty, and holiness.

A Theology of the Psalms, A Walk of Faith

In the context of the beautiful language of prayer and poetry, we discover the entire Gospel message, prophetically proclaimed in the saving history of God's people. In fact, the whole story of the Bible, from Genesis to Revelation—from creation to God's final glorious reign—is captured in these Scriptures. The Psalms beautifully reveal God's story with his people—a calling, a rebellion, a gracious reunion—not just in ancient Judea and Palestine, but for us today. They trace a path of salvation through our Lord Jesus Christ. They speak the story of our lives.

The movement of our walk with God can be mapped out in the Psalms, as a pattern. The Psalms prove not only useful, but encouraging and hopeful, as we navigate the phases and seasons of our faith. As they are grouped in this study[5], they track:

1. Our assent to God, his promises, and his ways (a spiritual high of discovery—an epiphany, if you will),

2. Our struggle to reconcile our experience with God in a broken world (a descent of sorts—a disconnect between God and the world—a Lenten movement), and

3. Our rediscovery of God as our only meaningful reality—a reconciled understanding of God (an upward Easter movement).

Whether we are new to faith or have been raised in it, we find ourselves somewhere on this path. This continuum of faith expressed in the Psalms may be stretched over a lifetime, or it may happen from one moment to the next, on any given day. The Psalms track our ups and downs, our confidence and our doubts, our times of despair and hope. *Pilgrim's Path: A Study of the Psalms* unfolds the wisdom and encouragement of the Psalms so that we may more faithfully traverse the path to which God has called us.

How to Navigate This Study
This six-week study is comprised of daily devotions to be accompanied by a weekly study. Each weekly study offers an online video teaching with additional material, insight, and reflection on the Scriptures. All three components—devotions, studies, and video teachings—are meant to function as a whole. *Pilgrim's Path: A Study of the Psalms* explores 48 of the 150 psalms included in the Psalter. This study does not endeavor to cover all the psalms. The devotions and studies are divided into categories based on major themes recognizable throughout the Psalter. Pilgrim's Path: A Study of the Psalms can be studied independently or as part of a group. To begin the study, I recommend you listen to the video session, *An Introduction to the Psalms*. (biblestudymedia.com/pilgrimspath).

I pray as you engage this study and the richness of the Psalms, you will discover the path is delightful, stimulating, challenging, surprising, and full of joy. You do not go alone. The Lord Jesus Christ goes with you. May he bless you and draw you to himself through this time in his Word.

"I run in the path of your commands, for you have set my heart free."

PSALM 119:32, NIV

Daily Devotionals

Each week introduces a category of psalms to teach key facets about God and our relationship with him. The Daily Devotions introduce each set of psalms, one psalm at a time, helping you delve deeper into the Scriptures and discover biblical connections. Each set of weekly devotions is ordered and designed to be read before interacting with the corresponding Study Guide sessions. The devotions serve as a foundation to support the key points of the Study Guide session. If you read all seven devotions each week before engaging with the appointed psalm in the Study Guide, you will be well-prepared to understand the concepts.

How to Begin

1. Set aside time to spend with the Lord each day.
2. Pray and ask the Lord to reveal himself to you through the pages of his Word.
3. Read and reflect on the appointed psalm for each day.
4. Complete the Study Guide session once weekly.
5. Use the Study Notes space to record verses that strike a chord, as well as ideas that are new or relevant.

As you do these things, the Lord will surely be present to you and bless you with the riches of his Word.

WEEK 1

PSALMS OF
CREATION

Introduction to Psalms of Creation

The first session of our study introduces the Creation Psalms. We like them because they lift us up out of the mundane and show us heights and vistas that come from our relationship with God, the Creator. They expand our souls—like a beautiful walk in nature, a day by a mountain stream, a night under the stars. While the psalms try to capture the glory of God's creation, they are not meant to romanticize nature but to glorify God, who made everything by his word. Everything God made is to reflect his glory.

As we meditate on God's creation, as these psalms lead us to do, we encounter the character of God. We get to know him as we ponder his work, much like we can understand an artist by reflecting on his artistry. We see his power, his creativity, his order, his righteousness, his faithfulness, and his love. In addition, we see how the character of God is instrumental in holding together all he has created. By his presence and activity in the created world, all creation thrives.

Just as elements of creation reflect God's character, we, too, are meant to display God's glory. The Creation Psalms show creation in relationship with the Creator and uniquely cast a vision for our role in the landscape. The more we understand the nature of God, the more we understand our purpose and who we are called to be. It is God's creation that sets the stage for the bountiful and sacred experience we call "life," and which is most fully expressed in us through Jesus Christ.

DAY 1

BEHOLD ME

Read Psalm 19.

It is easy to look into the vast expanse of the sky and wonder about the design of the heavens and the earth. Whether considering the expanse of the endless blue skies from a mountaintop or gazing at the rising moon in a summer night sky, one ponders ideas that only prompt more questions. We want to know measurements—how far away the stars are, where the universe begins and ends. We wonder about the relationships between the stars, moons, and planets, and also humankind's connection with them. How do all these elements hold together? We marvel at the beauty and power of a lightning storm in the black of night and how a gentle amber dawn brings reassurance in the hours that follow. For all our unanswered questions, there is a regularity, a certain continuity evidenced in the skies. Celestial patterns continue day in and day out, night after night. There is comfort in the fact that each new day the sun will rise again. Yet even the sunrises and sunsets press on our curiosity. Everyone, everywhere, in every generation, has marveled at the sky and wondered what more there might be.

Psalm 19 teaches us that the heavens themselves give us hints at the answers. They point to something much larger than our concept of "sky." They are like a riddle that asks, "What is immeasurable, infinitely beautiful and powerful, continuous, full of order, and known universally throughout time?" The skies invite us to see something greater than the obvious in front of us. They draw our minds to think of *Who* or *What* has created them.

In the first verse, the skies "declare"—proclaim, make a bold statement, make an accounting of—the glory of God. In other words, the skies express the nature of God. The word "glory" is a complex term meaning many things. One meaning is *to make something recognizable.* "Glory" is an aspect of God we can see. At any given time, glory is his holiness, goodness, and his radiance on display for us. Therefore, the physical attributes of the sky help us see aspects of God so that we can know something about him.

The skies proclaim the handiwork of God—the work of his hands. One very important distinction evident in the Creation Psalms is the difference between the Creator and the created. The extraordinary majesty displayed in the sky is not meant to be the focal point; the One who created them is. On my walk by the bay each morning, I often say, "Isn't the sky glorious this morning?" Yet the psalmist asserts that it is not the sky, but the One who made it, who is glorious.

The sky reflects God's glory. God is the Creator, and what he makes reflects his glory.

The Creation Psalms establish the idea that we can know something about God by studying his creation. I have in mind the image of an artist who expresses himself in his craft. "This is how you can know me. See what I have fashioned with my imagination and my hands. This is an expression of *me*." But think for a moment: if God made the skies, and the skies declare his glory, then God must *intend* to make himself known through them. Throughout the Bible, God is constantly taking the initiative, interjecting himself, showing up on the scene, disclosing himself in a myriad of ways in the natural order—through rain, fire, the hush of the wind, a raging storm, through animals, birds, fish, and insects. *"I was ready to be sought... I was ready to be found... I said, 'Here I am, here I am!'"* (Isaiah 65:1). The first verse of Psalm 19 speaks to the self-revelatory nature of God. He is constantly putting himself on display in the most obvious ways so that we might catch a glimpse of him, and wonder about him, and experience wonder *in him*. Remarkably, he does it through something as universal and transcendent as the skies.

This declaration of God's glory is poured out abundantly—spilling over, pooling up everywhere. There is no place throughout the earth where the voice of the resplendent sky is not heard. It is not bound by language, nation, tribe, or race. It is known by rich and poor, powerful and weak, educated and illiterate, devout and skeptic alike. That is the whole point. God created a landscape, an arena, where everyone, everywhere, would have access to his glory with the hope that they would be caught up in it with God himself.

The mysteries and wonders of the sky open our minds to the possibilities of something outside of our finite existence—something we cannot see or touch, something immeasurable and continuous. The celestial spread above us teaches that power, beauty, majesty, awe, and even danger can be intertwined. Exhilaration comes by being wide open to it, and yet a refuge is needed. The heavens and the skies stretch the limits of our imaginations. They challenge our perceptions, proving we can never answer all our questions! Yet, they show us something new every day! God's glory is on display before our very eyes. Do we have the eyes to see it?

*"Lift up your eyes on high and see:
who created these?
He who brings out their host by number,
calling them all by name,
by the greatness of his might...*

~

*Have you not known? Have you not heard?
The Lord is the everlasting God,
the Creator of the ends of the earth."*

ISAIAH 40:26, 28

REFLECTION:

Can you think of a place in nature that has completely captivated your attention because of its beauty or serenity? Rather than thinking of adjectives to describe the place, how would you describe God, who made it for you?

DAY 2

POWER AND PROVISION

Read Psalm 104:1–18.
I have a favorite spot, high up on a mountainside, a little scramble off the hiking trail, where I like to sit and reflect on the beauty of God's creation. From this perch, I can see a long, continuous line of snow-capped peaks that form the range in which I sit. I can watch the clouds form, dark and ominous, over the western peaks and wonder at the coming storm. Above me, not far from the summit, is a set of massive boulders stacked upon themselves, threatening the gentle valley below. God's power is so obvious in the mountains. It is seen in a sudden hail storm, the force of a river carving a gorge out of the rock, an avalanche that scalps a forest. I look up at the boulders that hover above me, but I am not unnerved. I am at peace under their shadow. What brought them to this spot? What holds them in place? There seems to be a boundary they do not pass (v. 9). For whatever reason, they are restrained, perhaps for millennia. Power—a restrained power—is part of what we know about God by studying his creation.

In Psalm 104, I have the sense the psalmist has also situated himself in a lofty perch where he can survey a majestic scene. His description sounds much like the opening chapters of Genesis with the progression of light, the formation of the heavens, then the earth, the oceans, vegetation, and then the birds and beasts, and finally mankind (v. 1–15). The psalmist is not as impressed with the physical scenery as with the action of God behind it. There is an intense force at work that cannot be thwarted. *"He set the earth on its foundations"* (v. 5). *"The mountains rose, the valleys sank,"* as God appointed them (v. 8). Waters fled at his rebuke (v. 7). This account speaks of dynamic, unparalleled power.

Power alone can be a dangerous trait. In Psalm 104 and throughout the Scriptures, God's power is used for provision, for the benefit of creation. *"Springs gush forth in the valleys"* for every beast of the field to drink (v. 10). Branches are made for birds (v. 12). God *"causes the grass to grow for the livestock and plants for man to cultivate,"* trees for birds' nests, mountain slopes for goats, rocks for badgers (v. 14–18). God has thought of every detail needed to provide for all he has made. God provides with a power that works for the good (Romans 8:28). The psalmist says, *"When you open your hand, they are filled with good things"* (v. 28). This is how God interacts with what he has created. He is powerful and beneficent in nature.

God's power and provision are also designed to bless. *"The earth is satisfied"* by God's hand upon it (v. 13). God quenches the thirst of the wild beasts. The birds sing from the branches. To be quenched is to be satisfied. To sing is to be at peace. Trees are abundantly watered; the stork has a home and a badger a refuge. Abundance, a homeplace, a refuge are the hallmarks of a heart deeply satisfied. Plants and animals are not just for food and sustenance but to gladden, anoint, and strengthen the heart of mankind. This blessing is for all creation. God's powerful hand at work satisfies us.

From my outcropping on the mountainside, I think of these verses as I study the delicate pink petals of a wild rose growing from underneath the rock. A chipmunk carrying an acorn in his mouth scurries across my path. Perhaps he hears the "caw-caw" of the hawk, still circling in the skies above. All this beauty, sustained in perfect harmony by a powerful hand! Yes, Lord. *"The earth is satisfied with the fruit of your work"* (v. 13). God sustains everything with his creative power and his generous inclination to fill everything with his goodness. As Paul said to the Greeks long ago, *"In him we live and move and have our being"* (Acts 17:28).

We know all this on a mountaintop. It is obvious, when we are engulfed in the natural splendor that speaks of God in every breath. From this vantage point, there is no argument that what God gives to his creation is more than enough to satisfy our hungry, agitated, restless, weary souls. How we long to be quenched, to sing, and to dwell side by side in safety, to find our home which is also a sanctuary, and to be gladdened by the work of our hands. Psalm 104 sketches a portrait of who God is and his intended relationship with all he has made. It is good. It is all very good.

> *"[Jesus] is the image of the invisible God... by him all things were created, in heaven and on earth, visible and invisible... and in him, all things hold together."*
>
> **COLOSSIANS 1:15–17**

REFLECTION:

What powerful acts has God performed in your life? Make a list of the things God has provided that sustain, strengthen, and delight you. Do you trust God to provide for what will truly satisfy you?

DAY 3

BOUNDARIES

Read Psalm 104:19–35.
There is something very comforting and hopeful about the sunrise each morning. I wake up early almost every day, make my way in the predawn light, and find the path along the bayfront where I hope to catch the inaugural event. Light seeps across the horizon, like molten gold oozing over the water's edge. At first white-hot and formless, the emergent sun finds its proper outline and begins its ascent. Day has dawned. The sun appeared on schedule, just as I expected. Time to begin again.

Psalm 104 tells us that when God made the world, he set parameters and established an orderly pattern in it. We see evidence of this everywhere. The sun rises every morning, after every night. Spring comes again after winter, new shoots after barren branches. There is a regularity in the world that attests that life is not random or chaotic. Apples fall downward in gravity. The earth rotates at a certain speed. Steam forms from water at 212 degrees Fahrenheit. These limitations help us to know more about the world. We can calculate, expect, and forecast. The foundations of civilization are based on these parameters. With the orderly rotation of the sun and moon come seasons, produce, commerce, science, art, and even religion.[6] Something so ordinary sets everything in motion. We grow, eat, work, and thrive. We beget. We discover, delight, and believe. That is the way the world goes around, from the beginning of time.

The nineteenth verse focuses on the establishment of the sun, the moon, and the stars, cataloguing the work of Genesis 1. With them comes the idea of time. But time is only measurable within boundaries—beginnings and endings. We are so quick to shrink from the idea of boundaries, as if they are limitations on our lives, as if they restrict our freedom. And yet, these verses teach us that boundaries set the stage for a life that flourishes. By the sun, we know when to rise and work, when to plant, grow, and reap. By the moon, we know when to rest and be refreshed. The inherent order of the universe provides the structure by which we thrive.

In God's structured landscape, there is abundance. The earth and seas are replete, providing for everything in due season. *"The earth is full"* (v. 24). The sea teems (v. 25). All gather (v. 28), again a reference to the abundance of Genesis 1. Yet, today's culture is more apt to view creation from the cursed version of it in Genesis 3. *"In pain you shall eat of [the ground] all the days of your life; thorns and thistles it shall bring forth for you; and you shall eat the plants of the field. By the sweat of your face you shall eat bread, till you return to the ground"* (Genesis 3:17–19). As a result of the fall of man, we are born to struggle. We make a habit of fighting—against creation and sometimes the God who made it. We work when it is time to rest. We burn the candle at both ends. We eat and drink more than our share. We hoard today's resources or consume them conspicuously, as if provision might run scarce. We expend ourselves, testing the boundaries, driving ourselves to exhaustion, illness, frustration, or disillusionment. Only then do we discover we are out of sync with the way God made us to enjoy his creation. In God's ordered universe, he gives, and we gather (v. 28). It is critical that we remember this sequence and reorder our lives accordingly.

Patterns are embedded into the spiritual realm as well as the physical. We encounter God's provision, abundance, and well-being in our spirits. When God's Spirit is upon us, we are created anew. We are inspired. We are filled up. When we are separated from God's Spirit, we expire. We are nothing but dust (v. 29–30). This is a spiritual reality. Just as one sows in the Spirit, one reaps life. If one sows to please his own natural desires, he reaps destruction (Galatians 6:7–8). This is the order of the spiritual realm. Life lived under the pattern of the Spirit flourishes.

God's spiritual order does not restrict us or limit us. It frees us. *"The Lord is the Spirit, and where the Spirit of the Lord is, there is freedom"* (2 Corinthians 3:17). Jesus said the Spirit of the Lord was upon him (Luke 4:18–19). If we bind ourselves to Jesus and his teaching, he promises a life that is truly free (John 8:36)—free from the struggle and fight into which we were born. When we know the love of Christ, we will be filled with all the fullness of God and learn to live abundantly (Ephesians 3:19, John 10:10). God sends forth his Spirit, and by it we are renewed (v. 30)!

God gives us patterns in nature so that we will recognize his reliable patterns in our spirit. Nature is a prototype of what he is doing in us and for us. He is as regular and consistent as the sunrise each morning. God shows up again and again, day after day. He is still here. Just as the rising sun brings a new day, his Spirit brings new beginnings. With the dawning of each new day, we can expect God's goodness to fill our lives, as he has filled the earth. It is a pattern he has established from the beginning of time and brought to us through Jesus, our bright morning star, who has risen (2 Peter 1:19).

REFLECTION:

What patterns or boundaries in your life have brought blessing and fullness? Is there anything in your life that is out of order or out of bounds, that causes you stress, frustration, or suffering?

DAY 4

THE PERSONAL POWER OF GOD

Read Psalm 145.
The Creation Psalms guide us to ponder God's unsearchable greatness (v. 3) and meditate on his splendor and majesty (v. 5). They take us to the high vistas where we think BIG, complex thoughts about God. No wonder God shows us aspects of his character in things like the sky, the mountains, the patterns of seasons, and everything that surrounds us. We can understand God better by seeing him in motion. It is easier to see God in the natural world than in the day-to-day rhythm of our lives. Where is his power at the end of a difficult work week, in a lost job, a struggling marriage, a hard decision, a sick loved one? In Psalm 145, we encounter a God who is in motion for his people.

In this Creation Psalm, David focuses on God's personal engagement with his creation. God's greatness is best understood by his "mighty acts," "wondrous works," and "awesome deeds" (v. 3–6). He describes God's character by using the same words God used for himself in Exodus 34:6: *"The Lord is gracious and merciful, slow to anger and abounding in steadfast love"* (v. 8). These qualities can only be known by what God does, by seeing them in action. God is merciful; therefore, he has mercy on all that he has made (v. 9). He is gracious; therefore, he opens his hand to every living thing (v. 16). He is righteous; therefore, he is good to all (v. 9). He abounds in steadfast love; therefore, he raises up all who are bowed down (v. 14). As a parent bends in strength to pick up his child, so is God's love for us. His love is tender, compassionate, restoring dignity and honor, providing strength and comfort in times of need. Who God is (his character) and what he does (his actions) are the same. So, when we declare God's character, we must also be looking for that action in our lives.

Too often, we do not see God's power because we are looking for a material impact—the needed promotion, the improved health diagnosis, the changed behavior in a loved one. We want to see change happen like lightning in the sky—an outward display that is clear, immediate, and definitive. More often, God's work is internal, in our spirits. His first and primary concern for our well-being will be in the spiritual realm, through his acts of love, mercy, and forgiveness. Yes, his power provides for our needs. But it will be intensely personal.

God made it personal when he sent his Son. *"For God so loved the world, that he gave his only Son"* (John 3:16). The love, compassion, mercy, and righteousness that God wanted to pour into his creation was acted out by his Son, Jesus. Jesus came for all who would believe in him. He came down to pick us up (Philippians 2:5–7). In his compassion, he bore our wounds upon himself, and in his mercy, he died on the cross so that we would be healed (Isaiah 53:4–5). In God's strength, he was raised from the dead to new life (Ephesians 1:19–21). He embodied the Father's character perfectly and completely. In so doing, we are raised up too. That is how the Father loves us, by raising us up (v. 14).

So, you see, it is not enough to say that God is love. We must see his love at work in our lives. It is not enough to say that God is powerful, but to see his power changing us inside. His power is his love. It radically changes our lives. If we want to see his power, we must be looking for it in his love.

The psalmist says that all of God's works will declare his mighty deeds of power throughout the generations (v. 10–12). What stories about God will we pass down to our children? I do not think they will be about a lightning storm or a sunrise. I do not think they will be about houses, jobs, or degrees. The stories we tell about God will be about relationships—about changed hearts. They will be about how the love of Jesus had the power to change lives for love and glory. Now, that is a powerful story!

REFLECTION:

Below are some of the character traits of God listed in Psalm 145. Next to each trait, describe a way God has acted this trait out in your life.

Gracious:

Merciful:

Slow to Anger:

Abounding in Steadfast Love:

Faithful:

Kind:

Righteous:

DAY 5

THE SPLENDOR OF HIS HOLINESS

Read Psalm 29.
Have you ever stood in the center of a storm? Have you ever felt the wind whip your face and sheets of rain drench your hair? There is something pure about a storm. It is raw, untamed, and somehow truthful. It blows away pretensions, facades, the temporal shelters we put in place. A storm strips us of superficialities and leaves us bare—completely real, completely ourselves.

In Psalm 29, we are standing in a storm. It is the movement of a holy God over and through his creation. He is a powerful force, raw and untamed. The psalmist traces the path of the storm as it moves across the turbulent waters, hitting the shoreline, breaking the cedars, then moving inland, shaking the desert with its power, and stripping all in its path. We discover again a landscape where everything and everyone is subject to the power and glory of God. But this time, we find that the awesome and formidable scene is, in its entirety, the temple of the Lord (v. 9). We have entered a holy place, where God is exalted completely and unequivocally. He is lifted up and enthroned over it all (v. 10). All of creation is the temple of the Lord, and all creation bows down before him.

The opening acclamation of the first verses fits the scene. *"Ascribe glory... ascribe glory and strength... worship the Lord in the splendor of his holiness"* (v. 1–2). We are standing on holy ground. We are made to worship God everywhere he is present. It is God's holiness that makes every place sacred. Like a great antiphonal liturgy, the voice of the Lord rings out over creation, and we have only one response: "Glory!" (v. 9). All creation will bow before the Lord as it acknowledges the glory of the Lord (Philippians 2:9–11). There is no dissent. The voice of the Lord is dynamic; it shakes the rafters, all tremble before it—but we remember that the voice of the Lord also creates (Genesis 1). Standing in his presence, we welcome his creative power. We cry for this untamed but true presence to sweep over us and create us anew.

The angels[7] are called to join in the chorus that nature has already affirmed, and in which God's people have their part, too (v. 1, 11). The call is to worship the Lord in his holiness. What is his holiness? There is no one like God in all of creation. He is completely set apart from his creation. As Creator, he stands outside of creation. He is not made. Isaiah tells us that God's holiness is also a combination of his righteousness and his justice (Isaiah 5:16). He is completely pure and true. There is no imperfection or stain in God. No evil is present in his character or behavior. His holiness is all goodness, purity, and truth.

But who can stand in his holy presence (Psalm 24:3)? God's holiness comes with power like the storm. In it, our imperfections and weaknesses are exposed. Our faltering foundations are ripped up. All that can be shaken is shaken (Hebrews 12:25–28). What remains is holy, that which is truly of God. Now, left standing alone at the center of the storm, still we cry "Glory!" because now we are truly ourselves before God. Paul tells us to present ourselves—open and vulnerable—before the Lord, holy and acceptable (Romans 12:1). This is our act of worship.

When we worship the Lord, we enthrone him (v. 10). He is exalted, lifted up, victorious over all our circumstances. We ascribe to God alone our whole being, frail and faulty as it is—lay it on the altar, and we are changed. When we might expect fire to consume our sacrifice completely, we find it has instead been blessed (v. 11). He has accepted another sacrifice in our place. Christ, our Passover Lamb, has been sacrificed for us so that we may keep the festival (1 Corinthians 5:7–8).

In the grips of God's holiness, we discover that God has turned our storm to peace (v. 11). Strengthened by the storm, we lift our voices with angels, archangels, and the whole company of heaven and forever sing: "Holy, Holy, Holy Lord, God of power and might. Heaven and earth are full of your glory. Hosanna in the highest. Blessed is he who comes in the name of the Lord. Hosanna in the highest."[8] Let the storm come.

REFLECTION:

Is there something you would like to offer to the Lord as a sacrifice upon his altar, that he may burn away its impurities and then bless it utterly?

DAY 6

HE WHO FASHIONS HEARTS

Read Psalm 33.
Psalm 33 presents another account where the power of God's word is unmatched and commands the attention of all creation. The psalmist recounts the progress of creation, beginning with the heavens and the stars, then the gathering of the waters and the deep. But as if we already know the Genesis story, the psalmist makes a quick leap over the subsequent phases of creation to his subject of primary interest: mankind. Psalm 33 defines how we relate to God.

Just as God fashioned the heavens and the earth, gathering them to their places and designing their function, so God fashioned a people for himself (v. 15). By the same word and breath (Spirit) by which God made the heavens and the stars (v. 6), he also made mankind. *"God said, 'Let us make man'... and breathed into [man's] nostrils the breath[9] of life and the man became a living creature"* (Genesis 1:26; 2:7). In that act, we were made like him. Something of his Word and Spirit is deeply fixed into our being. We correlate to God.

The Creation Psalms have been making the argument that God's imprint is on creation, the work of his hands. In the same way, Psalm 33 shows us the correlation between God and mankind, also the work of his hands. God said, *"Let us make man in our image, after our likeness"* (Genesis 1:26–27). So, if God is upright and righteous (v. 4–5), he has also fashioned an upright and righteous people (v. 1). In God's perfectly ordered creation, humankind is made to reflect God's righteousness, faithfulness, justice, and love.

There is a beautiful expression used by the apostle Paul in Ephesians 2:10. He says we are God's "workmanship." We are his handiwork. I have heard it translated "masterpiece." The original Greek word is *poiema* or poetry. We are made to be the expression of God's heart and mind, fleshed out in living lyrics that speak to the world the nature of God. Through us, the whole world should be able to see and praise the upright and loving God, joining in the joyful song (v. 1–3). The Scriptures teach us that there is a universal and eternal song of praise that is sung throughout creation, by angels and all creation (Psalm 148:2–12; Revelation 4:8–5:14). God designed us to sing his magnificent poem of salvation in a world that is frustrated, war-torn, filled with false hope, and plagued by death (v. 16–19). The lyrics to that poem are born in our hearts by God's Word and his Spirit.

Sometimes it seems we have lost the poem in the daily toil, the heavy burden, the empty promises and philosophies the world offers to us. But the song is still waiting for us. We can sing because a righteous people is being raised up for a righteous God. We are it! For *"I am sure of this, that he who began a good work in you will bring it to completion at the day of Jesus Christ"* (Philippians 1:6). God's word is upright (v. 4), and Jesus, the Righteous, is in us (1 John 2:1). Through his work on the cross, we are counted in the number of the righteous. By his Spirit, we remember the lyrics born in us (John 14:26). God has fashioned our hearts for himself, and he is faithful to complete his work in us. Let us join with shouts of joy, for the Lord has made us by his Word and filled us with his breath (Spirit) so that we may sing his song.

"I will not leave you as orphans; I will come to you…

~

In that day you will know that I am in my Father, and you in me, and I in you…

~

These things I have spoken to you while I am still with you. But the Helper, the Holy Spirit, whom the Father will send in my name, he will teach you all things and bring to your remembrance all that I have said to you. Peace I leave with you; my peace I give to you."

JOHN 14:18, 20, 25–27

REFLECTION:

What word do you want Jesus, the Righteous, to speak over you? His word is victorious and over all things (Revelation 19:11–16).

DAY 7

SOVEREIGN RULE, GLAD HEARTS

Read Psalm 33.

As we reconsider Psalm 33, we are intrigued by what a sophisticated and complex poem it really is. Our first look at the psalm focused on God's power by Word and Spirit to create not only the physical world, but specifically the hearts of his people. It highlighted God's righteousness, justice, faithfulness, and, above all, his steadfast love. We discovered with joy that we are made to be like God. We hold these facets in one hand, as we now consider Psalm 33 from another angle. We are altogether unlike God. Psalm 33 makes this important distinction, giving us a new perspective on God's sovereignty and the blessing it brings.

In his commentary, *The Message of the Psalms*, Walter Brueggemann writes, "there is a deep inequity between Creator and creation."[10] As much as we are like God, made by his Word and Spirit, modeling elements of his character, we are also completely unlike God. God the Creator stands above and over all he has created (v. 13–14). He is not subject to the bounds of creation as we are. Humanity is utterly temporal, subject to famine (v. 19), wars (v. 16–17), and death (v. 19). God stands outside of time, providing counsel forever to all generations (v. 11). In terms of power and strength, mankind may employ strategic skills (v. 16–17), but we are powerless compared to the Lord, who needs only to speak to create (v. 9). Only God has the power to save souls from death (v. 17, 19). Psalm 33 reminds us there is a great disparity between us and our Maker.

This variance between our natures shows up in every human organization and society. God is completely sovereign over individuals, families, peoples, governments, and nations. There is nothing he made which rules over him. God makes his plans, and no power can thwart them—no foreign ruler, no despot, no charismatic leader (v. 11–12). God brings the prideful plans of mankind to nothing (Isaiah 40:23). The arrogant and self-important philosophies are brought to nothing, compared to God's counsel, which stands forever (v. 11). In times of turmoil and division, it is easy to rely on a military's arsenal, a president's agenda, or a politician's smooth promise. Psalm 33 offers true wisdom: *"The king is not saved by his great army; a warrior is not delivered by his great strength. A war horse is a false hope for salvation, and by its great might it cannot rescue"* (v. 16–17). It is futile to place our hope in the politicians and power brokers of the day. They bring nothing but false hope, for they cannot truly rescue or save. God alone is sovereign over our nation, our city, our family, and our lives.

Nothing can successfully challenge God. He frustrates the plans of all that are opposed to him (v. 11). This force is inherent in his sovereignty. Yet there is evidence of a proactive and positive force at work in Psalm 33—a force "for" his people. God chose people to be the recipients of his good, just, and loving rule. *"Blessed is the nation whose God is the Lord, the people whom he has chosen as his heritage"* (v. 12).[11] As his children, we are always under his watchful care (v. 13, 18), and because of his steady, unwavering love for us, he will deliver us, always (v. 19).

So what do you fear? What rattles you when you read the daily news, study the financial markets, consider political elections, hear reports of the health epidemic or increased military threats? Psalm 33 reminds us that God is in control over it all. God's sovereign rule is one of our greatest blessings. We should delight in his rule. He does not just rule over nations, but also our hearts. His sovereignty means that fear does not have to dominate our lives or our outlook for the future. We must look at God's power this way: If he is completely in control, and he loves us, then we have absolutely nothing to fear. *"If God is for us, who can be against us? He who did not spare his own Son but gave him up for us all, how will he not also with him graciously give us all things... Who shall separate us from the love of Christ? Shall tribulation, or distress, or persecution, or famine, or nakedness, or danger, or sword?... No, in all these things we are more than conquerors"* (Romans 8:31–32, 35, 37).

How foolish we are to forget we are not God. How frustrated we become when we take our worries and the problems of the whole world upon our shoulders, seeking to have them all sorted out on the commute home, before we pick up the kids from school, get homework started, and figure out what's for dinner. God is sovereign over it all—everything we carry in our hearts and on our backs. We can give it all to him. Let us be like the psalmist and wait in confidence and hope for the Lord, trusting completely in his love and power to save, so our hearts might be glad in him.

> *"Come to me, all who labor and are heavy laden, and I will give you rest. Take my yoke upon you, and learn from me, for I am gentle and lowly in heart, and you will find rest for your souls. For my yoke is easy, and my burden is light."*
>
> **MATTHEW 11:28–30**

REFLECTION:

In what way does the idea of God's sovereign power over your life comfort or bless you? In what ways does it challenge you?

NOTES

WEEK 2

PSALMS OF

TORAH, WISDOM, AND WELL-BEING

Introduction to the Torah, Wisdom, and Well-Being Psalms

It is a great wonder to discover that the majestic, transcendent God of Creation speaks to us. We are not left to glean knowledge of God through elements of his natural creation, only guessing at his purposes. Through the Holy Spirit, God inspired his Word, both spoken and written, through men and women throughout every age, until he completed and fulfilled it in his Son, Jesus Christ. Through the Holy Scriptures, we are given an audience with the heart, mind, and Spirit of God. This section explores three kinds of psalms: Torah Psalms, Wisdom Psalms, and Psalms of Well-Being. Together they create a well-defined path for our lives, leading us into the presence of God.

The Torah Psalms (psalms about God's Word and Law) teach us the value and purpose of engaging intimately with the Holy Scriptures. They reveal the blessing of adhering to God's Word and the assurance of freedom, confidence, peace, joy, and life. They train us how to live in the fullest and truest expression of ourselves, primarily through Jesus, the Living Word.

The Wisdom Psalms teach us how to order our lives according to God's patterns in creation. There is a method and structure for humankind to thrive in God's well-ordered world. The Wisdom Psalms help us understand the biblical ideas of "wisdom" versus "foolishness" and the importance of discerning the difference.

The Psalms of Well-Being express the fullness and blessing of a life well-lived according to God's design. They articulate the abundant life designed for us under God's gracious canopy of love, righteousness, justice, and sovereign rule.

DAY 8

GOD'S WORD

Read Psalm 119:1–89.
If I wanted you to know something of great importance, I could make a diagram for you to study. I would draw it out with my own hand, taking care to highlight particular aspects of my message. I would mark it with arrows and make broad underlines. If I wanted to draw your attention to it, I could clash cymbals near the diagram. I could set flashing lights over the illustration to catch your eye. Successful in my measures, I would find you perusing it, casually at first, then more carefully. Fascinated, you might spend time studying the intricacy of design and the harmony of colors. Turning it sideways, you would see something different altogether, a whole new aspect. Day after day, I'd catch you draped over the diagram, with your elbows on the table, your chin in your palms, studying, pondering all the possibilities, even taking notes for yourself. You might invite others to look at it with you. And they would ask, "But what does it mean?" Because it is so beautiful and so complex, there must be many possibilities. It baffles you at times, as much as it delights you. Perhaps I could make a key to the diagram. I could write a set of instructions to accompany the picture. But if I really wanted to convey my valuable message to you, I would come alongside you and tell you myself.

So we find ourselves, in God's wide and beautiful landscape, in his magnificent diagram, trying to understand the One who made it. But what does it mean? To our utter marvel, we discover that he has made a key or a set of instructions for us. Through the inspiration of his Holy Spirit, men and women throughout the ages heard, felt, and experienced God in such a way that they wrote the event into words. Stories, poetry, histories, songs, dreams, visions, and letters—all written down to help us understand what the intricate and complex scene around us means. This is how God chose to speak in the early days. God's Word tells us directly his message of great import. Through his Word, God tells us about himself.

Psalm 119 affirms that God's Word is a true and accurate representation of God. As we read, we discover that God's Word is righteous (v. 7, 75), is good (v. 39, 68), speaks love (v. 41, 76), gives hope (v. 49), is trustworthy (v. 86), and is eternal (v. 89). As we immerse ourselves in God's Word, we surround and saturate ourselves with his personality, much like we do in nature, except with more clarity. It is a special revelation of God, as opposed to a natural one. God's Word is a manifestation of his character. It is a key to his mind and his heart.

When we read novels or autobiographies, we gain insight into the author. This is certainly true in reading the Scriptures. But there is something much more. Because God's Word is inspired by the Spirit and a true expression of God's nature, it carries God's power. As the writer of Hebrews wrote, *"The word of God is living and active"* (Hebrews 4:12). The Greek word *energés*, translated "active," means "effective, powerful, able to produce a result." It penetrates our souls, judges our hearts, and uncovers us before God. Something is opened up inside of us when we encounter the living, active Spirit of God in his Word. God's Word has the power to effect a change in us. We cannot remain the same.

The psalmist hopes and prays for such transformation. He prays for his eyes to be opened (v. 18), to be strengthened (v. 28), to understand (v. 34), to turn (v. 37), to speak with authority and confidence (v. 46), and yet to exhibit love and mercy (v. 76–77). The change will be dramatic and obvious to others (v. 74). Look carefully at the transformation. The psalmist's personal attributes begin to align with God's. God's Word is doing nothing less than saving him (v. 41, 81). The psalmist declares that God's ways set his heart free (v. 32 NIV) and give him hope (v. 49), so he can *"walk in a wide place"* (v. 45) with a song in his heart (v. 54). In short, he is learning to live the abundant life God has designed for him. (v. 25, 40, 50). And it delights him! Such is our experience with God's Word. It opens us to the Spirit of God, and we are changed.

God delights to save us, fill us with his presence and attributes, and bring us life. Is this what the Artist of the magnificent diagram wanted us to know? Would we know this just by looking at the trees swaying in the wind? Would we know his purposes by studying the clouds form on the distant horizon? Perhaps, perhaps not. But this knowledge of God and his plan is only a beginning. For a key to the diagram can still be misunderstood or skewed. We might have the whole thing upside down. For us to truly get the whole picture, God is going to have to come alongside us and tell us himself. And so he did. And so he does.

> *"In the beginning was the Word, and the Word was with God, and the Word was God. He was in the beginning with God. All things were made through him, and without him was not any thing made that was made. In him was life, and the life was the light of men.*
>
> ~
>
> *And the Word became flesh and dwelt among us, and we have seen his glory, glory as the only Son from the Father, full of grace and truth.*

*For from his fullness we have all received, grace upon grace.
For the law was given through Moses;
grace and truth through Jesus Christ."*

JOHN 1:1–4, 14, 16–17

REFLECTION:

In what ways does God show you he loves you through natural creation?

In what ways does God show or tell you he loves you through his Word?

In what ways does God show you he loves you through his Son Jesus?

DAY 9

HOW THEN SHALL WE LIVE?

Read Psalm 119:90–176.
In our study of Psalm 8, we were given a glimpse of God's glorious idea for mankind. Like an addendum to Genesis 1 and 2, it summed up God's majestic decree for our lives—a noble calling to a life of honor and glory. It rightly prompts us to ask, "How do we do this? Where do we begin? How can we know the way?" Psalm 119 tells us the answer. We are to begin with God's Word.

Psalm 119 is a summary of all the benefits of God's Word for the intent and purposeful follower. Psalm 119 is a blueprint of God's Word, showing us the way to God, helping us navigate the course even when it is marked by obstacles and dangerous detours. It leads us to a life of peace, abounding in God's ever-present love. The life God intends for us begins by understanding his promises and learning to live by his statutes.

The psalmist uses the image of a path to illustrate that God's Word leads us not simply to a standard of living, but to God himself.[12] God's Word shines light on the path, gives direction, and keeps us steadily going in the right direction (v. 105, 130, 133). God's Word protects the pilgrim along that path (v. 114). But there are detractors trying to steal, distract, and derail us from the glorious goal (v. 115). We can get lost in the din of voices that suggests we pursue our own way (Genesis 3:1–7). So the psalmist rightly turns to God's Word for sustenance and rejoices in it. *"Uphold me according to your promise... hold me up, that I may be safe"* (v. 116–117). God's Word keeps us oriented rightly to God's righteous character and to God himself (v. 137). When we adhere to God's way, we are near God (v. 151).

God's Word is completely true, trustworthy, and brings wisdom. Therefore, we do not walk blindly or without knowledge of where we are going. God's Word is true in several ways. First, it lines up perfectly with the character of God. It conveys his righteousness (v. 137), love (v. 76, 132), mercy (v. 156), wisdom (v. 98, 99), faithfulness (v. 90), strength (v. 115–117, 170), judgment (v. 118–119), light (v. 105, 130) and life (v. 93, 116, 154). Because it is true to God's nature, God's Word can be trusted. It will not fail us or offer false hope. God's Word works (v. 140). Therefore, God's Word is true in a second sense. It represents a reality that God has built into his creation. What God says, happens. Just as he spoke in the beginning of creation, so it happened. *"So shall my word be that goes out from my mouth; it shall not return to me empty, but it shall accomplish that which I purpose and shall succeed in the thing for which I sent it"* (Isaiah 55:11). Thirdly, God's statutes are true, in that they never change or waver, like a math sum. They are as constant as he is (Psalm 102:24–27, Hebrews 13:8). The psalmist emphasizes that God's Word is eternal (v. 144). It goes on forever. It has stood the test of time (v. 152). It has been applied to real lives in generation after generation, and its truth has been attested. God's promises have been tested, and the psalmist asserts they bring peace, hope, salvation, delight, and life. Because God's Word is consistent with God and reflects the enduring ways and patterns built into creation, it brings us wisdom. We can know his truth and apply it to our lives. We can discern right from wrong, truth from lies, wisdom from foolishness. We can walk our path with confidence and integrity.

God's Word brings life and love. It is the path to the life that God designed for us. That life is characterized by peace (v. 165), salvation (v. 155), joy (v. 111, 162) and delight (v. 92, 174). God's rules and statues are not restrictions but promises for abundant life (v. 154, 156). Moreover, all these benefits are the product of God's love. *"Give me life according to your steadfast love"* (v. 159). Out of his love, God desires to show us the real and true way to live. As we follow, meditate, pursue, remember, cherish, and keep his statutes, we find ourselves like the psalmist, wrapped up in praise for God (v. 164), full of joy (v. 162), full of hope (v. 166), and peaceful and confident (v. 165), with a soul completely open to God (v. 167–168). Such is the life God decrees us.

It is no surprise that when the disciples asked Jesus, *"How can we know the way* [to the Father]?" the Word made flesh answered them, *"I am the way, and the truth and the life. No one comes to the Father except through me"* (John 1:14; 14:1–6).

REFLECTION:

What decision or circumstance are you facing that could use the direction, wisdom, or understanding of Jesus?

Which verse in Psalm 119 speaks a promise to you, concerning your circumstance above? Pray that promise to Jesus and ask him to fulfill it in you. (You may use the space below to write out that prayer.)

DAY 10

BLESSED

Read Psalm 1.
The first psalm begins with a powerful word of encouragement. "Blessed" is the one who delights in the law of the Lord (v. 1). Opening the Bible with a commitment to learn and grow is to begin a journey marked by favor, honor, and acclaim. The opening acclamation captures our attention with a promise that awaits us.

Before we can receive the promise, we are presented a challenge. The psalmist introduces our incumbent blessing with a warning. There is a choice to make, for there are two ways to go, and only two. Blessed is the one who delights in God's ways. They will experience all the goodness inherent in God's universe. All others will perish. Those who separate themselves from God's law of life will find only death. We stand at a crossroads. Just as Moses counseled those who were about to enter the promised land, we too are faced with a choice as we begin our journey. *"See, I set before you today life and prosperity, death and destruction. For I command you today to love the LORD your God, to walk in obedience to him, and to keep his commands, decrees and laws; then you will live and increase, and the LORD your God will bless you in the land you are entering"* (Deuteronomy 30:15–16, NIV). As we read the psalms, we are introduced to a landscape promised to us from the beginning of time, a good and pleasing place, full of blessing and abundance (Genesis 1:27–31; 2:8–9).

The dichotomy presented in Psalm 1 pervades the Psalter and is present throughout Scripture. There are two kinds of people: the righteous and the wicked (or the foolish). It is uncomfortable language to our modern ears, bent toward inclusivity and compromise. We tend to temper distinctions—even through the eyes of grace—between those who seek God and those who do not. While we remember that we personally cannot judge what is hidden in others' hearts, the Scriptures are clear. There are only two paths: one which turns towards God, and one which turns away from him.

The two paths illustrate a pattern that shows up everywhere in God's creation. God has woven his character traits into the universe. When we live in accordance with his character, life will go well for us. Likewise, a life lived apart from his character foolishly invites hardship and frustration. This is God's moral law. It applies to the universe just as physical laws apply. In grace and love, God chose to reveal this law to us through his inspired Word. This Word or law (*torah* is the Hebrew word for "law") is our guide to the life God has for us.

So, our choice lies in this: will we take our counsel from God's Word or from some other influence in our world around us? What will govern our lives going forward? It is a decision point. Will we seek the company of those who scoff at God? Will we fill our minds, ears, and eyes with material that calls evil good? What will influence, shape, and mold our lives? Is it in sync with God's ordered creation? It is an important decision. Our choice will play out in every facet of our life, for better or worse.

The psalmist, to help us in our decision, forms a picture for us. Should we choose God's way, we shall be like a tree planted by streams of water (v. 3). Securely planted and purposefully nurtured by God, our life will be watered and refreshed by his Spirit (John 7:38). We will develop in faith, into our fullest potential, yielding mature gifts that are ripe and sweet. And though we age, our vitality will not falter but strengthen over time (v. 3; Psalm 92:14). The broad, lush branches of our life will stretch wide to offer shade and rest for others, and many will be drawn under their protection. Generations will call us blessed.

Let us press on together, remembering Moses's own word of encouragement:

> *"But the word is very near you.*
> *It is in your mouth and in your heart, so that you can do it."*
>
> **DEUTERONOMY 30:14**

REFLECTION:

On a scale of 1 to 5 (1 = never, 5 = regularly/all day/multiple times a day), how much time daily do you spend consuming the following?

A.	News articles from mobile device, TV, or newspaper	(1 2 3 4 5)
B.	Magazines, catalogues, or websites (Pinterest) with new ideas about clothes, home décor, outdoor gear, etc.	(1 2 3 4 5)
C.	Celebrity news from print or digital tabloids	(1 2 3 4 5)
D.	Facebook, Instagram, or other social media	(1 2 3 4 5)
E.	Movies or serial programs on Netflix	(1 2 3 4 5)
F.	Spiritual/biblical devotionals	(1 2 3 4 5)
G.	Actual verses from the Bible	(1 2 3 4 5)

How do the things you fill your mind with affect how you think or act?

Do you see an opportunity to trade out one or more of these activities for more time engaging with God's Word? How would that change your daily, or even hourly, perspective?

DAY 11

GOOD THINGS HAPPEN

Read Psalm 112.
If someone asked you to make a short list of behaviors that lead to success, what would you include? Even if you have never written out this list, you have probably conveyed it in other ways—in loving instruction to your children or sage wisdom to a young protégé. You might include things like: be honest, work hard, persevere, be generous, forgive easily, be kind. Maybe this advice was handed down to you. For it is generational wisdom that people who conduct themselves according to these principles are successful in their ventures.

It is broadly understood that those who practice honesty, who are trustworthy and show kindness, are usually well-liked and develop genuine friendships. Those who work hard, persevere, and delay self-gratification in pursuit of higher goals achieve their objectives. Those who practice forgiveness, who are kind and merciful, who are generous, find it comes back to them exponentially. When we pour out our lives for others in love, we receive love in return. These types of actions align with God's moral universe and reap a predictable outcome—blessing, joy, fulfillment, and peace. Galatians 6:7–9 puts it this way: *"A man reaps what he sows. Whoever sows to please their flesh, from the flesh will reap destruction; whoever sows to please the Spirit, from the Spirit will reap eternal life. Let us not become weary in doing good, for at the proper time we will reap a harvest if we do not give up"* (NIV).

Psalm 112 presents such a list to us, that it may go well for us. The psalmist depicts the behaviors of a righteous person who fears God and the positive outcomes that are his reward. These promises are for those who follow God's law. What are the traits of a righteous person according to Psalm 112? Let us make a list. A righteous person:

- delights in God's commands (v. 1),
- is gracious (v. 4),
- is merciful and compassionate (v. 4),
- is generous (v. 5),
- is just (v. 5), and
- gives to the poor (v. 9).

The righteous person distinctly reflects God's attributes, which he has learned and acquired through applying God's Word (v .1). As we are learning, good things happen to people who fasten themselves to God's good ways. Let us look again at the list the psalmist provides. Here are the promises for the righteous person:

- The blessing is carried down through the generations—multiple generations are blessed (v. 2).
- Wealth and riches result (v. 3)*.

    Special note on the topic of wealth and riches: If taken in a material sense, the blessing of wealth and riches is very characteristic of Old Testament promises. However, we know some of the greatest saints are often the poorest. Additionally, in our poverty, we can know a richness about God that cannot otherwise be known. Spiritually, we know that the spiritual wealth and riches afforded to us in Christ are unequalled by anything earthly. What riches can rival a heart at peace with itself and God? So do not think this goes down the "prosperity gospel" route. Nor is this a salvation according to merit. It is a pattern of blessing. Uprightness is often the road to success and all other things being equal, "an honest person is a rising person."[13]

The blessings continue for the righteous person, not as material blessings, but in confidence and security. The righteous person:

- lives in light (v. 4),
- is never shaken or rattled (v. 6),
- will be remembered (v. 6),
- is secure in mind and heart, not afraid of the future (v. 7–8),
- will be honored (v. 9).

These blessings are core to our self-identity, confidence, and security of our soul. These blessings are priceless and cannot be measured. So, we can say with the apostle Paul, *"Now to him who is able to do immeasurably more than all we ask or imagine, according to his power that is at work within us, to him be glory"* (Ephesians 3:20–21, NIV).

As we study these characteristics and behaviors, we see another pattern developing—a very attractive and valuable trait. The person portrayed is a person of integrity. "His insides line up with his outsides." What he believes is reflected in what he says and does. The person of integrity is in sync with the way God has fashioned and formed her, and therefore fits into his creation seamlessly. She is made in the image of God and orders her conduct according to that image. Are we not the happiest and most content when we are doing what we are made to do?

Jesus was the most fully integrated person to ever live. His entire character, actions, and aspirations were completely aligned with the purpose of God. Psalm 112 could be a portrait of Jesus. He, too, taught on this subject. The way to fulfillment and blessing in this life is to follow the path of righteousness. *"But seek first the kingdom of God and his righteousness, and all these things will be added to you"* (Matthew 6:33). He also said, *"Blessed are those who hunger and thirst for righteousness, for they shall be satisfied"* (Matthew 5:6). And yet, as always, Jesus takes it one step further. The satisfaction Jesus talks about does not come from material or even spiritual resources. It comes from God. When we seek God and his righteousness, we will be filled with God and his righteousness. God satisfies us with himself, specifically through Jesus. In God's goodness and love, he made Christ Jesus to become our righteousness so that we might have the fullness of God (1 Corinthians 1:30; Ephesians 3:19). Thanks be to God! Good things happen to people who seek after a good God.

> *"For our sake he made him to be sin who knew no sin, so that in him we might become the righteousness of God."*
>
> **2 CORINTHIANS 5:21**

REFLECTION:

Make a list of all the blessings you can think of in your life that are a result of God's goodness to you.

DAY 12

A FOOL'S ERRAND

Read Psalm 14.
"Oh, the tangled web we weave when we practice to deceive." Perhaps you heard this homespun proverb as a child. It is a lyrical way to teach a moral lesson. There are others too. "Cheaters never prosper." These axioms instruct us that dishonest acts like lying, cheating, and stealing create more problems than they fix. Dishonesty begins in small and innocuous thoughts and acts which compound in weight and severity over time. Most of us learned these truths when we were young. One or two failures secured a modest measure of wisdom in our small worlds. Yet we still encounter those who think they can evade these common truths. These sayings remind us that there is a moral order in God's universe. Actions contrary to God's character result in ever-increasing frustration, degeneration, and evil. Those who persist in them, even with initial success, can only be seen as completely foolish or resolutely evil.

The Psalms have a very clear definition of the "wicked" or "foolish" person. Psalm 14 puts it simply, *"The fool says in his heart, 'There is no God'"* (v. 1). The psalm also shows the direct progression from foolishness to wickedness (v. 3–4). Fools turn aside from the Lord. They become corrupt because they have a distorted understanding. They cannot do good because they no longer know what is good. They never learn, so they persist in their practice. Prone and conditioned to evil (the only alternative to good), they do evil. As a result, God is not with them (v. 5). In Psalm 37, another Wisdom Psalm, the wicked will be cut off from the Lord. The outcome for the wicked is a transient existence (37:2), separation from God (37:9), and death (37:20). These psalms illustrate and illuminate the consequences for those who willfully turn from God.

Surely everyone has behaved foolishly at one time or another. There are perhaps many times that we can assign the phrase, "What a fool I was," to a past behavior. It is easy to see in retrospect that we did not seek God's ways in every decision. Or perhaps we knew God's ways, but consciously turned aside. Maybe we were too wise in our own eyes (another trait of foolishness according to Proverbs 12:15 and 28:26). Quite plainly, we thought we could handle it on our own. It would be nice to chalk it up to immaturity. Some of us have had to learn wisdom the hard way, by experience. Turning from God's good order and design has disastrous consequences. God's Word contains helpful, even loving admonition. Be careful of foolish behavior. It has a downward spiral.

The apostle Paul tells us in Romans 1:21 that when we give our minds over to foolish thinking, our minds become "futile," eventually "darkened," and ultimately "debased."

> *"And since they did not see fit to acknowledge God, God gave them up to a debased mind to do what ought not to be done. They were filled with all manner of unrighteousness, evil, covetousness, malice. They are full of envy, murder, strife, deceit, maliciousness. They are gossips, slanderers, haters of God, insolent, haughty, boastful, inventors of evil, disobedient to parents, foolish, faithless, heartless, ruthless. Though they know God's righteous decree that those who practice such things deserve to die, they not only do them, but give approval to those who practice them."*
>
> **ROMANS 1:28–32**

Only the fool thinks that she is not vulnerable to such behavior. Only the fool thinks that he will not be held accountable. But we are and will be (Romans 3:10–20). Our thoughts and actions have consequences in God's moral universe. He will judge all the motives of our hearts, the work of our hands, the good and the evil. If he did not, he would not be good at all, and the fool would be no fool. But we do not have to wait for the end of time to know the outcome. We already know those who suffer under these practices. They are lonely, empty, fearful, and paranoid. They are pitiable. The life they choose is no life at all.

Do not be fooled, says the psalmist. The wicked who laugh at God, dismiss the warning, and intentionally pursue their own path will find a "great terror" (v. 5). How much they want to chart their own course—for pleasure, for license, for power. What fools they are! For somewhere along their cruel and heartless journey, the wicked will find themselves fearfully fighting against an undefinable and horrible dread that has overtaken their souls.[14] They will earn life without God—a judgment they have called upon themselves.

The psalm closes on a hopeful, even joyful note, much needed at the end of four brutally honest verses. For the psalmist has drafted a sketch of the "fool," "the wicked," at first seemingly far removed from ourselves and then all too inclusive. *"There is none who does good, not even one"* (v. 3). The psalmist casts the hope of salvation in verse 7 for the poor fool who wrestles against God and himself, a brief reference to Jacob (Genesis 32:22–30). He can change our name from "trickster, scoundrel, cheat" (Jacob's original identity) to "God contends with me," and even "people of God" (Israel's new identity). God in his love and grace has a plan to bring us into righteousness—his righteousness. Salvation has come out of Zion. His name is Jesus.

REFLECTION:

Why is it important that God judge the whole world fully for all thoughts and actions (Matthew 16:27, Romans 2:1–11)?

What if evil (small or great) was not punished?

By what standard do you think God should judge the righteous and unrighteous?

DAY 13

THE LAW OF LOVE

Read Psalm 15.
"O LORD, who shall dwell on your holy hill?"

Psalm 14 set us up for this penetrating question. Psalm 14 built a case for the questionable condition of our hearts before a righteous God, and then told us the answer would come from Zion, God's mountain. Perhaps David, the psalmist, is wrestling with his own heart before the Lord and wants to set an orderly account for himself before God. Or perhaps something more practical and expedient was on his mind. Scholars believe both Psalm 15 and Psalm 24 reference the time King David brought the ark of the covenant back to Jerusalem, with much celebration, worship, and festivity. The ark was the gilt container built to house the stone tablets engraved with the Ten Commandments, and where God promised to dwell and meet with Moses on behalf of the people (Exodus 25:10–22). This would be David's first real encounter with the ark itself. The history of the ark carried with it numerous accounts of those being struck dead because of their unrighteousness or disobedient actions pertaining to the ark.[15] So perhaps these disastrous encounters were on David's mind. The issue at hand was the holiness of God and the unholiness of God's people. And yet, the ark (and the law) issued an invitation—the opportunity to abide with God. Would God condescend to dwell with David? Or any of us?

It is an important question for every believer to contemplate. Who is fit to enter the presence of the Lord? Do we ever ask that question? Put another way, who may fellowship God and on what basis? The question alone conveys a sincere and earnest desire to be in God's presence. No wonder in 1 Samuel 13:14 and again in Acts 13:22 the Holy Spirit calls David "a man after [God's] own heart." David's sensitive and inquiring heart asks the question in the first verse and proceeds to answer it in the ones that follow.

The psalm asserts that only someone who exhibits the character of God can dwell with God. Only the one who is blameless and does what is right, who speaks the truth from his heart and does not slander with his tongue, who does no evil to his neighbor will be able to sustain fellowship with the Lord (v. 2–3). A person who honors and protects the innocent and the poor, and who faithfully keeps promises even at his own cost, such is the person that can enter the presence of God (v. 4–5). Charles Spurgeon writes, "We must be like him, or we shall never be with him."¹⁶ This is the message of God's Word, or God's law. It is a guided path to grow in the character of God.

When Jesus was asked which was the most important commandment in the law, he said this:

> *"'You shall love the Lord your God with all your heart and with all your soul and with all your mind and with all your strength.' The second is this: 'You shall love your neighbor as yourself.' There is no other commandment greater than these."*
>
> MARK 12:30–31

How closely Jesus's summary mirrors the words of Psalm 15 and portions of the Ten Commandments (Exodus 20:12–17). In fact, Jesus was summarizing the Ten Commandments—the basis for the Torah—the Jewish law. The first four commandments are about loving God. The remaining six are about loving your neighbor. But with a little more thought, it also reminds us of Paul's great teaching on love. For is not the operative word in Jesus's response "love"? Let us compare Psalm 15 with Paul's description of love.

> *"Love is patient and kind; love does not envy or boast; it is not arrogant or rude. It does not insist on its own way; it is not irritable or resentful; it does not rejoice at wrongdoing, but rejoices in the truth. Love bears all things, believes all things, hopes all things, endures all things. Love never ends."*
>
> 1 CORINTHIANS 13:4–8

Paul began that passage by saying that he would teach his disciples a "more excellent way" (1 Corinthians 12:31). Rabbi that he was, he was still teaching them the law, but from a new perspective. For it is nothing less than a law of love. The law that God has built into the universe, by which we are to know and have life, is a law of love. The law that perfectly reflects God's character is a guided route to love because God is love. So when we talk about obeying God's law, we are talking about learning to love God, each other, and ourselves. Perhaps David has told us this much already. Those who will dwell with God must love like God. Love your neighbor as yourself. This is the answer to his imperative question.

Jesus spells it out for us in another way:

> *"As the Father has loved me, so have I loved you. Abide in my love. If you keep my commandments, you will abide in my love... This is my commandment, that you love one another as I have loved you. Greater love has no one than this, that someone lay down his life for his friends... You are my friends if you do what I command you."*
>
> **JOHN 15:9–10, 12–14**

REFLECTION:

Read through Psalm 15 again, studying each requirement in verses 2–5. Is there something you could do better to serve or love your neighbor? Now turn to 1 Corinthians 13:4–8. Where do you find encouragement to pursue this action?

Offer this action (and perhaps your specific "neighbor") up to the Lord and ask for his indwelling Spirit to help you love more fully.

DAY 14

THE PEACEABLE KINGDOM

Read Psalms 131 and 133.
We have been building a picture of God's kingdom thus far. We have studied God's character, our special role in creation, and his expectations and counsel for an abundant life, all of which lead us to the Psalms of Well-Being. These psalms express the fullness and blessing of a life well-lived according to God's design, a life at peace with God and others. In Psalms 131 and 133, we see that kingdom living is best expressed by loving God and loving our neighbor.

As we enter Psalm 131, we discover that we have trespassed upon a deeply personal, deeply intimate conversation. What a beautiful picture of a man—a warrior, a leader, a king—who quietly bares his soul before his God. Quickly we discover that his posture before God is one of humility and submission. *"O LORD, my heart is not lifted up; my eyes are not raised too high; I do not occupy myself with things too great and too marvelous for me"* (v. 1). Though he is king and superior in authority, power, and wealth (presumably) to all around him, he does not think of himself more highly than others, nor does he look down on others. He understands his position before God, which is the only one that seems to matter to him. "It is not a relationship among equals."[17] He is content in the sphere where God has placed him, not seeking his own accolades or self-promotion, not trying to impress others. What restless energy we expend seeking a place not (or not yet) appointed to us. His understanding of his proper relation to God, and therefore his place in the world, is part of the wisdom which leads to his peaceable state.

In contrast to the agitated, discontented life of one wanting too much for oneself, David has calmed and quieted his soul (v. 2). Like a weaned child on his mother's breast, no longer crying or demanding, the psalmist is at peace in the intimate presence of the Lord. Fulfillment, satisfaction, rest, and comfort come not from what we are given, but by the presence of the Giver alone. It is a picture of intimate love, satisfied love, on both parts. Is this the picture Jesus had in mind when he said, *"Love the Lord your God with all your heart and with all your soul and with all your mind and with all your strength."* (Mark 12:31), when nothing else vies for our attention but the heartbeat of the Lord?

Psalm 133 takes this same yielded, humble heart and directs its love outward to community. *"How good and pleasant it is when brothers dwell in unity!"*

This is a community—a family, no less—that is at peace with itself. Any parent can attest to the inestimable value of siblings at peace with each other. It can be downright pleasant. But, whether within the small context of a nuclear family or the greater scope of a spiritual family (like the church), it is easy to divide over the smallest details. Politics divides. Theology divides. Economics divides. Race divides. Nationality divides. The list becomes increasingly specific and tedious and is seemingly endless. We can divide until there is not a single determinate whole left, only fractions of people, families, cities, and nations. Jesus said, *"If a kingdom is divided against itself, that kingdom cannot stand. And if a house is divided against itself, that house will not be able to stand"* (Mark 3:24–25). He knew that Satan seeks to divide us at every turn, on every issue. So we must recognize the utmost importance of unity to the well-being of our families, our country, and the kingdom of God.

One of the key goals and accomplishments of Jesus's life, death, and resurrection was to create a new community of people that transcended social, racial, economic, and gender delineations. Christians—fellow believers from every tribe, nation, and language—have been coming together ever since to *"love one another"* (John 15:12). It works. The powerful love of Jesus binds people together in a way that nothing else can!

Love is *"like the precious oil on the head, running down on the beard, on the beard of Aaron, running down on the collar of his robes"* (v. 2)! It is rich, fragrant, smooth, seeping into all the pores. It is the kind of love that blesses, anoints, and heals. It is extravagant in measure, pouring and pooling all over those in our circle that need it most. *"It is like the dew of Hermon, which falls on the mountains of Zion"* (v. 3)! Thick and damp, like the morning dew in the mountainous heights. Like wading through the wet grasses and woody shrubs on the high slopes, drenching your hemline, socks, and shoes, so is the refreshment of God's love shared. It is meant to cover us from head to toe.

Love does have a cascading effect. God pours it out and over us, as a mother does to her child. It changes us. We are finally quiet in our spirit, at peace with ourselves and God. We pour this same love out on others, who need his refreshment so desperately—like smooth oil on dry skin, like fresh dew in an arid land. It changes them, too. No one can stay the same. Love makes something new possible. The love of Jesus changes every human organism, first with a single heart, then rippling outward to a family—brothers, sisters, aunts, uncles, cousins—then encompassing friendships, widening to neighborhoods, gaining cities, and spreading to nations. There is more than a hope for a world of peace. It is not wishful thinking. Love happens. God's beautiful peaceable kingdom is at hand. It has already begun. It is time to take our place in it. Therefore, let us love the Lord our God with all our hearts and love our neighbor as ourselves.

REFLECTION:

Can you think of relationship where you felt the unity of God's Spirit and love so much that it became a model for another relationship—either with a new acquaintance or the next generation? Describe.

NOTES

WEEK 3

PSALMS OF LAMENT

Introduction to the Psalms of Lament

We have been identifying the attributes and benefits of God's orderly creation and how we fit into it. Our study has explored the sense of well-being and blessing often reflected in the early stages of our spiritual walk with God. Trail markers are clear, the way is discernable, and all is well. The Psalms of Lament introduce us to a new phase—a period of disorder and disarray. It comes unexpectedly, turning all we know upside down, causing disorientation. Such disorientation can be caused by loss, confusion, betrayal, grief, upheaval, death, and countless other things that shake the foundations of our lives. Suddenly the way is imperceptible, as is God. The Psalms of Lament question our understanding of God and our relationship with him.

While the Psalms of Lament show discontent with the change of status, they are also acts of faith. They express an intimate relationship with God that is painfully honest, vulnerable, and genuine, even in crises. Our honest cries, pleas, and complaints reveal a more accurate picture of our faith that can either falter or strengthen. If we choose to cling to God, we discover new attributes that only suffering, pain, and the reality of sin in the world can teach us. We also discover more intensely the power and love of God who sent his Son Jesus to enter our suffering, bear our sin, and ultimately free us from it.

DAY 15

HOW LONG, O LORD?

Read Psalm 13.

Things are not as they should be. Up is called down. Good is called evil. Lies are called truth. What we see going on in the world today is not a distorted reality TV series meant to entertain. It is not a story on the nightly news in a town far away from you and me. Marriages are breaking up. Teenagers are dying from drug overdoses. Friends sink into alcoholism. Powerful politicians escape justice. Government officials accept bribes. Children watch pornography. Adults prey on them. This is real life. It happens every day before our very eyes, in our neighborhoods, in our homes. Things are not as they were designed to be. The world is broken, and God's moral universe is under attack. There is an existential problem threatening us all, but for David it is personal.

David laments an indeterminate and unnamed enemy in Psalm 13. By all outward appearances, the enemy is gaining ground. The unrighteous prosper by their self-appointed rule over the righteous. It is indeed an opposition attack on the kingdom of God. What perplexes David is the seeming absence of God, for surely God would not allow the wicked to exalt themselves over the righteous. So, while his personal status may be under attack (v. 3, 4), David's real sorrow and anguish come from a disorientation, a disconnect with God himself. Things are not as they should be. David is missing the personal pleasure of God's presence in his life—which he recognizes by God's powerful acts, always consistent with his loving goodness. When those are missing, is God still there? This is a question we all ask when suddenly it seems the blessing of God has been removed.

"Consider and answer me, O LORD my God" (v. 3). What an intimate, immediate prayer! It is as if David takes the Lord by the shoulders with a forceful grip and says, "Look at me, talk to me!" The prayer is not one of doubt. Just the opposite. Convinced that God is present and alert, David pivots in his prayer. *"Light up my eyes."* Let *me* see you! Show yourself to *me*! If God would but turn his face, his light would shine on David so he could see through this dark hour (Numbers 6:24–26). David does not doubt that God is present; it is only that he cannot see God at work. It is a faithful prayer. How much it reminds us of Paul's prayer, *"that the eyes of your heart may be enlightened in order that you may know the hope to which he has called you, the riches of his glorious inheritance in his holy people, and his incomparably great power for us who believe"* (Ephesians 1:18–19, NIV). When we cannot see God at work or we think his rule is under siege, we can still pray this prayer of faith. *"Light*

up my eyes," so that we may know the hope that is ours through Jesus, and his power that is at work in the world.

Psalm 13 is a beautiful expression of faith in God. Though the enemy is at the gates, and our hearts are rattled, this psalm teaches us to trust in God's character above what the circumstances assert. David is confident that God will not allow the enemy to "prevail" or let the "foes rejoice" over him. He renews his trust in God's most foundational character trait—his steadfast love and his signature act of power, salvation (v. 5). God is always loving us and saving us, moment by moment, day by day. Though the enemy endeavors to shake our faith, God's love cannot be shaken. As we cling to it, we stand on firm ground. God's promises are firm, he will lift up the righteous and restore their fortunes (Psalm 126:1–3). Remembering God's character and power restores David's trust in God's goodness, not just as a general understanding, but a personal affirmation. God has been good to *me*! And so he sings. The prayer which began in tears and sorrow, alone and isolated from God's presence, has ended in a commitment to praise and sing about God's love and goodness. This change in perspective can only be the answer to the prayer in verse 3, *"Light up my eyes."*

Let us join with David against the enemy, not with fear and trepidation, but with confidence and song. The enemy is not new, nor is he original. With eyes of faith wide open, we will see God act upon all the promises he has made to his righteous people. Indeed, he has acted. The light of the world has stepped into our dark places (John 8:12) and brought his saving, resurrecting power to all that seems lost ground or given up for dead (v. 3; Ephesians 1:19–20; John 11:25–26). God will right the wrongs. The truth will be told. Evil will be judged. He will turn the world right-side-up. God will fulfill, through his Son Jesus, all his promises to bless, exalt and honor the faithful people who wish to see his face (2 Corinthians 1:20–21). Trust in the Lord's unshakeable love, and sing because he saves. God has dealt bountifully with us.

REFLECTION:

What are some of God's loving and saving acts in your life—things that cannot and will not change despite your circumstances. Make a list. Then say (sing?) a prayer of thanksgiving and praise for his unshakeable love towards you.

DAY 16

INSOLENT MEN

Read Psalm 86.
In Psalm 86, David is faced with an attack from an outside enemy. Typically, when faced with a crisis, we rush to our arsenal of ideas and tools to assess where we stand. We assess the potential threat, our available resources, and strategies for resolution. In Psalm 86, we see such an orientation. David begins his prayer by making an accurate and fair account of the assets at his disposal and what he will need to successfully thwart the crisis. From this warrior king comes an excellent example of prayer made in perfect solidarity with God.

The enemy in Psalm 86 is a band of *"insolent men"* (v. 14)—arrogant and ruthless—who has risen up against David and God. Rather than flailing in chaotic confusion, David begins by assessing the strengths at his side (namely God) and the potential threat and list of weaknesses (the enemy and his own abilities). As if taking inventory, he catalogues God's attributes. God is inclined to hear (v. 1), gracious (v. 3), good and forgiving (v. 5), abounding in steadfast love (v. 5), responsive to prayers (v. 7), and far superior than all other gods or powers (v. 8, 9). In turn, David records his own strengths and weaknesses. He is poor and needy (v. 1), only a servant (v. 2), one who can only call for help and cry out in trouble (v. 3, 6–7). He is a single entity attacked by a band of many (v. 14). He is hated and hunted (v. 14, 17). Those are the threats and weaknesses. However, he is also one who trusts God (v. 2), lifts up his soul (v. 4), and inclines himself to learn the ways of the Lord, walk in truth, and unite his whole heart to God (v. 11). Those are his strengths. David has a clear awareness of who God is and his position before God. Every prayer needs to begin with this understanding.

Far from being ambitious and self-motivated, David prays in a way that shows a completely integrated relationship with God. Read carefully the interplay of pronouns throughout the psalm: you and I, me, my, and yours. The exchange between David and his God is like a dance in which the two are completely entwined. David is establishing that they are a unit. They are a pair, a duo, a team. David asserts, *"You are my God"* and [I am] *"your servant"* (v. 2). He prays in utter sweetness, *"unite my heart"* to your name (v. 11). This is not a professional arrangement. David does not need a hired gun. They are in a personal relationship. Every time David mentions *"steadfast love"* (v. 5, 13, 15), he is reminding God of their covenantal relationship. It is a relationship sealed by love, commitment, and faithfulness.

David has made an excellent argument, more like a legal strategist, for God to hear his prayer. He presents the problem: *"a band of ruthless men seeks my life, and they do not set you before them"* (v. 14). It is twofold in nature. His life is at stake, and so is God's reputation. David is indignant that these insolents dishonor God. For David, his problem is God's problem, and vice versa. He has completed the delicate but fortified weaving of solidarity between the two of them. They are completely unified in purpose. They are allied forces. It is such a union that, while he continues to pray for strength (v. 16) and a sign (v. 17), David already knows the outcome. The band of men will be put to shame (v. 17). He has already received his help and comfort (v. 17). This is a powerful prayer that can bring calm, confidence, and hope into every crisis.

We can claim this same solidarity. It is ours through Christ. God has completely allied himself with us through his Son Jesus, who lived and walked in our fleshly humanity, knowing pain and suffering, humiliation and rejection. Jesus so identified with our problem of sin that he took it upon himself and died for us, only to endow us with his indwelling Spirit, after his resurrection and ascension. We can have the utmost confidence that our problem is his problem. In fact, he prays with us and for us (Romans 8:26; Hebrews 7:25) regardless of our eloquence, strategy, or confidence in prayer.

What is your crisis? Assess God's strengths. Offer your own. Confess your weakness. Ally yourself completely with God (which is called repentance). Present the problem to God. This is a winning strategy every time. He will bring you through it.

> *"Finally, be strong in the Lord and in the strength of his might. Put on the whole armor of God, that you may be able to stand against the schemes of the devil. For we do not wrestle against flesh and blood, but against the rulers, against the authorities, against the cosmic powers over this present darkness, against the spiritual forces of evil in the heavenly places. Therefore, take up the whole armor of God, that you may be able to withstand in the evil day, and having done all, to stand firm. Stand therefore, having fastened on the belt of truth, and having put on the breastplate of righteousness, and, as shoes for your feet, having put on the readiness given by the gospel of peace. In all circumstances take up the shield of faith, with which you can extinguish all the flaming darts of the evil one; and take the helmet of salvation, and the sword of the Spirit, which is the word of*

God, praying at all times in the Spirit, with all prayer and supplication."

EPHESIANS 6:10–18

REFLECTION:

Is it hard for you to praise and trust God during difficult circumstances? How might Psalm 86 help you focus your attention on God and not the problem?

DAY 17

WHEN A FRIEND IS NOT A FRIEND

Read Psalm 41.
The treachery has drawn much nearer. Rather than an assault from a nameless band of outsiders, the enemy has emerged from inside the trusted circle of friends. It was a breach of the sacrosanct. The wound leveled was subtle and sophisticated—no material harm occurred, no blood was drawn, no bounty stolen. In fact, the general civility with which it occurred seemed to make the offense even more egregious. A knife to the back, then slowly twisted. Nothing hurts more deeply than the dawning realization that a friend is not a friend. Such is the basis for David's lament in Psalm 41.

Psalm 41 is a human song. David wrestles with an injury he can hardly understand. Yet, he is intent to master his feelings and behavior despite the scandal of this vulnerable exposure. His prayer is specific about the offense. A trusted friend had access to him while he was sick, in a weakened state of body and mind, and used it against him publicly. Instead of compassion, his friend showed "malice" (v. 5). Instead of kindness, his friend uttered "empty words" (v. 6). While David was down, his friend gossiped and slandered him (v. 6–7). Here is what he cannot understand. *"Even my close friend in whom I trusted, who ate my bread, has lifted his heel against me"* (v. 9). Even "the man of my peace," as the original Hebrew reads. David expected friendship but received betrayal.

In contrast, David captures the friendship of God. *"The LORD will strengthen him upon the bed of languishing: thou wilt make all his bed in his sickness"* (v. 3, KJV). The picture is of a compassionate God at the bedside of the ailing David, intimately present, providing strength in mind, body, and spirit, even metaphorically fluffing the pillow and pulling up the covers to provide comfort. This is the friendship of the Lord our God. It is in sharp contrast to how David was treated by those he called "friends." Betrayal is so terribly disheartening. It completely crushes the spirit. And yet the presence of God sustains us with what others have withheld.

In struggling to understand the breakdown, David judges himself. What was his part? Did he deserve this treatment? David grapples with his own behavior and how to respond to the betrayer. He knows God's standard is mercy, and *"blessed is the one who considers the poor"* (v. 1). Mercy will be shown to the merciful (Matthew 5:7). No doubt he considers himself in this category, for he fully expects God's merciful rescue and restoration to health. Yet only God is truly merciful. His self-examination must quicken his spirit, for it leads him to confession (v. 4). Whatever his part in the failed relationship, he offers it to God. His pleas are for God's mercy only. *"O LORD, be gracious to me"* (v. 4, 9). To whom else shall he turn? A trust has been broken on all other accounts. How shall he, the king, repay this injustice (v. 10)? Psalm 41 is a complicated, honest, messy prayer that still clings to God when the outcome is unclear.

Here is David's dilemma. He has begun his prayer based on God's standard, which is mercy. It has driven him to consider his own character, which still leaves him at the foot of a merciful God. Even at the point of action, determining how to respond to the injustice, David can only move forward in keeping with God's mercy, or else he will jeopardize his integrity altogether. When we pray for God's direction, we are not at liberty to disregard it when he makes it known. David asks God to be gracious to him so that he may "repay" his enemy (v. 10). What do we suppose God's response is? The psalm does not say. What if David is to "repay" his enemy with the same grace he has been given? The psalm does not say that either. But we know that David concludes that his integrity has been upheld and he remains securely in the presence of the Lord (v. 12). This is God's response to his prayer. David is to remain focused on God's word and his presence. That is his reward. That is the grace. He must leave the rest to God.

It is natural to want to repay our enemies. Throughout Scripture, however, God asserts that *"vengeance is mine"* (Deuteronomy 32:35; Romans 12:19), and only he can judge and repay justly. And he will! In the meantime, are we willing receive the grace that God gives us? It is an essential question that underlies forgiveness. Will we accept what God gives to us, namely himself (v. 12), as sufficient payment for the debt owed to us by someone else? This is the question for each of us, each time we forgive. Will we accept the life of the Lord Jesus Christ as sufficient payment for the debt owed to us? He will take care of the rest. It is an issue of grace.

REFLECTION:

Has David's story ever happened to you? Have you ever been betrayed by someone close to you? Use the space below to analyze the event:

What did the person take from you?

What does the person owe you?

Is Christ's death enough to pay you for the wrong done to you?

Consider praying this prayer:

Jesus, I release _____ from any debt they owe to me. I receive your new life. Wash me and cleanse me from all the unrighteousness about this issue, which I have stored inside my heart. I look to you, Lord Jesus, to pay back to me what I am owed. I receive all the blessing that you want to bestow on me. In your name I pray. Amen.

DAY 18

WALLS CRUMBLING DOWN

Read Psalm 74.
Walls are razed. Pillars are strewn like broken bones. Smoke smolders where incense once rose. The gilt altar, vandalized and violated, is buried under the rubble but still holy in its task. It bears the blood of martyrs under the putrid ash. The scene the psalmist portrays is the desecration and destruction of the Jewish temple in approximately 587 BC. Now the enemy has a name. It is the marauding imperial army of Babylon. In Psalm 74, we are drawn into the great tragic grief of the people of Israel who have been attacked at the very core of their identity. The temple—the heart of Jerusalem, the heart of worship, the center of civic life—has been destroyed. The very place where God promised to meet and dwell with his people lies in a heap. How do we pray to God when our walls come crumbling down?

Civil and racial unrest have led to the desecration of churches and synagogues in our modern times. Wartime stories tell of the same sacrilege throughout history, in every age. But there are other walls that come down, other altars that are demolished. Grief is made of such events, when all on which we base our identity is suddenly removed. An athlete loses a limb. A mother mourns the death of a child. An honored reputation suffers a scandal. A minister falters in his faith. Often these incidents cause doubt in God, his promises, and even his existence. The walls that held up our lives have collapsed. But Psalm 74 is not a prayer of doubt. It is an insistent, passionate declaration of belief. It fervently grips God's promises and character, with no intent of letting go until God acquiesces to act. It is Jacob wrestling with God once more, until God relents to bless him (Genesis 32:24–29).

The psalmist is at once humble and bold, indignant and confident. He approaches God in humility, assuming the role of a chastened child whose lesson has been effective. He acknowledges God's wrath (v. 1) and recognizes that Israel is poor, downtrodden, and needy (v. 19, 21). Despite their lowly estate, they are still God's people, the *"sheep of your pasture"* (v. 1). "Your" is the key word throughout the psalm, attributing ownership to God. The psalmist makes a case that they are God's sheep, God's congregation, which God redeemed and called to meet in his meeting place on his mountain. "We are yours" which also makes them (and us) his cause. *"Arise O God, defend your cause"* (v. 22). The psalmist places God's fundamental promise of redemption and salvation before God himself (v. 2, 12). Will he withdraw his hand from the people he promised to save? The psalmist knows the answer, and so do we. Of course not! *"The LORD will fulfill his purpose for me"* (Psalm 138:8). So, he prays with boldness: Draw forth your hand (v. 11). The more the psalmist recalls the status given by God to the people of God, the bolder he becomes. God will act for his own cause. Finally, the psalmist expresses his indignation at the assault against God in hopes to raise God's own outrage. The attack is against God himself. The enemy scoffs at God and reviles his name (v. 10, 22). The psalmist prays for the namesake of God.

When our lives are threatened and our core is shaken, our prayers take on an intensity that shatters superficialities and drills to the heart of God's purposes. We must pray our strongest reasons.[18] No longer do we pray for the shallow or insignificant conveniences of our daily lives. No, we pray with fervor the core of God's character. We pray for redemption; we pray for salvation. We pray for God's name, not ours. How can he resist our prayers when they are joined to his? He cannot. Jesus promises that as we align ourselves with his purposes (and therefore God's), our prayers will be answered accordingly (John 14:11–14). These are the kind of prayers God has been waiting for us to pray. *"Our Father in heaven, hallowed be your name. Your kingdom come, your will be done, on earth as it is in heaven"* (Matthew 6:9–10). He always delivers on his purposes and always will. In our difficult circumstances, our prayers shift to join his.

Our heart-wrenched prayers offered from the turmoil of our lives teach us something remarkable and hopeful about God and ourselves. Firstly, we are still praying. That act alone shows our faith is still intact, despite the framework of our lives being in shambles. Moreover, we are praying at a deeper and truer level. It attests to the eternal nature of God in us and the depth of our connection to him. That which could be shaken has been removed so that what is eternal remains (Hebrews 12:27). Something about hitting rock bottom helps us find the foundation. Jesus, the cornerstone, is here at the foundation! The temple may have been destroyed, but it has been rebuilt in us (Ephesians 2:20–22). We can be confident that *"he who began a good work in [us] will bring it to completion"* (Philippians 1:6).

Whatever has been taken, stolen, burned, or desecrated in our lives, Jesus will rebuild in newness, holiness, and purity. Whatever remains from the wreckage, he makes eternal. Is it faith that needs to be rebuilt? Is it hope? Is it love? He is doing the work even now, as we pray in boldness for that same work. Lord Jesus, draw forth your nail-pierced hand and defend your cause.

*"When the perfect comes, the partial will pass away...
So now, faith, hope and love abide, these three;
but the greatest of these is love."*

1 CORINTHIANS 13:10, 13

REFLECTION:

What is something precious that has been lost to you? What is the eternal nature of it? At its foundation did it provide hope or love to you, or build up your faith?

Would you consider surrendering your loss completely to Jesus—as if it were a sacrifice on an altar to him—and pray for him to rebuild your heart with his eternal gift?

DAY 19

WORDS OF HATE

Read Psalm 109.
There is no rest from the assault of the wicked upon the righteous. In Psalm 109, we are confronted again with a desperate scene of the enemy encircling David like a pack of wolves ready to devour him. The enemy's sins are blatant and deserve full justice under the law. Equally apparent are David's emotions, keeping pace with his adrenaline. In this psalm of lament, David struggles to manage his hate, rightly demands justice for his enemies, and trusts the verdict that only God can give.

David quickly establishes the case against his foe. The wicked (either a single person or a vicious mob) speaks lies (v. 2), speaks hate without cause (v. 3), and returns evil for good and hatred for love (v. 5). Despite David's prayers and fasting amid this persecution (v. 4, 24), the onslaught persists. There can be no recourse but to announce this unrighteous action before God and the whole congregation. Verses 6 and 7 set the scene, with a ruthless prosecutor, the guilty standing trial, and the verdict already hanging in the balance. Guilty! David rushes to judgment and declares the forthcoming sentence—a heartless, cruel, and torturous penalty (v. 8–15). The wicked man and memory of him will be completely abolished. The punishment would be almost comical if it were not so vindictive. Do we hate like that? Do we wrap it around us like a belt we put on every day (v. 19)? Taking judgment into our own hands is a slippery slope. Jesus said, *"Judge not, that you be not judged. For with the judgment you pronounce you will be judged, and with the measure you use it will be measured to you"* (Matthew 7:1–2). Are we prepared for that?

Perhaps in wisdom, perhaps in desperation, David calls for the ruling of a righteous judge. *"But you, O God my Lord, deal on my behalf for your name's sake"* (v. 21). He concedes it is God's jurisdiction. Only God can rightly judge and rightly convict, because only God is truly just and good. Further, God attests that vengeance alone is his (Deuteronomy 32:35; Romans 12:19). David trusts in God's righteousness so completely that he can praise God for the outcome before it has come to pass. Leaving the problem in God's able hands (v. 27) ensures blessing and gladness (v. 28), thanksgiving and praise (v. 30), and salvation from the various graves we dig for ourselves. In short, the relinquishment of our rights to God brings us life.

Like a lawyer having made his concluding argument, David might as well be gathering his papers and files under his arm, preparing to leave the courtroom. The crowd disassembles slowly, trying to get a last glance at the shamed and scorned, waiting now only for the final sentencing by the true Judge. Somewhere in the restrained commotion, one hears a gavel. There seems to be one more statement from the Judge. "David," (I imagine he says, directing his penetrating gaze into David's eyes and soul), "I stand *'at the right hand of the needy one, to save him from those who condemn his soul to death'"* (v. 31). That is the final statement. But who is on trial now?

We are quick to seek judgment for our enemies from God. Yet strangely, he is quicker to give mercy. In Jesus, he does both, perfectly. For this, we must truly praise him! For with the same justice we seek for others, he will judge us also. "I stand *'at the right hand of the needy one, to save him from those who condemn his soul to death.'"* Our hatred is killing us. Our convoluted, twisted, self-righteous pre-judgment of others and ourselves makes a grave in which we bury ourselves alive. But in God's mercy, he sent his Son Jesus to bear the judgment and penalty for our sins upon the cross so we could live. *"For the wages of sin is death, but the free gift of God is eternal life in Christ Jesus our Lord"* (Romans 6:23).

When we are attacked and accused and wronged by another, we want to deal in wages. We want payment. But if we believe that Christ's death is just payment for the sin of the world, we can no longer justify our hate. We must relinquish to him any further recourse for payment or penalty for that sin. Therefore, Jesus calls us to forgive our enemies (Matthew 6:14; Luke 6:27–37). Not for their sake, but for his sake and ours. Forgiveness will be our freedom.

The righteous Judge has acted fairly on behalf of all parties related to this matter. He has addressed the case of the wicked. Whether they receive justice in this life or the next, God will handle our enemies (Revelation 20:12–13). He has also addressed the righteous. He has provided Christ the Righteous One (1 John 2:1) to do what we cannot do on our own—to bring us out of the grip of our enemy, out of the grave and into new life. *"With my mouth I will give great thanks to the LORD; I will praise him in the midst of the throng"* (v. 30). Justice and mercy have been served.

REFLECTION:

Have you ever tried to take things into your own hands when it seemed that God was silent? What was the outcome? What in this psalm changes your understanding about waiting on God to act?

DAY 20

DARKNESS

Read Psalm 88.

In Psalm 88, we enter a difficult dialogue. The tone and nature of the lament has become significantly more intense and desperate and concedes little hope. In this lament, we discover that the threat to the psalmist does not come from an outside enemy but from God himself. The psalmist directs his accusations toward God, who is silent. A strong image of death lays over the psalm like a pall, and the sense of abandonment by God is pervasive. There is a sad, tragic, disconnected nature to the conversation, which leaves us waiting in the breach, and we find ourselves at the end of the psalm sitting in utter darkness. Psalm 88 voices our most primal fear—complete abandonment, being left alone in the dark.

Psalm 88 prays in a way which we are often reluctant to do. Perhaps we do not know where it ends. Does it lead us to the end of our faith or to a new understanding? If Psalm 88 has any redeeming feature, it expresses what can often be inexpressible. In excruciating honesty, the psalmist accuses God of causing the pain he is in. *"You have put me in the depths"* (v. 6). *"Your wrath lies heavy upon me"* (v. 7). *"You have caused my companions to shun me"* (v. 8). Line after line, the psalmist lays his complaint before the Lord, effectively saying, "You did this to me." The circumstances are indeed dire, for the psalmist is clear that death is imminent. The images speak of hell (v. 3), the grave (v. 4–6), drowning (v. 7), and being buried alive (v. 8). His prayer, which clearly still contains an element of faith (v. 1, 2, 9, 13), lays the critical questions at God's feet:

> *"Do you work wonders for the dead?*
> *Do the departed rise up to praise you?*
> *Is your steadfast love declared in the grave?...*
> *Are your wonders known in the darkness?"*
>
> **PSALM 88:10–12**

In the end, isn't that what we all want to know? Has it got too dark for you to act, Lord? Has evil gone too far? Can we fall off the edge? Can we die apart from you? What if? What then? How can love coincide with the grave? These are honest questions, even if they are prayed in dire circumstances. They demand an answer.

The psalmist speaks our pain, *"O LORD, why do you cast my soul away? Why do you hide your face from me?"* (v. 14). Sometimes in our spiritual journey, we have to wait in the dark with no answer from God. We can be comforted that this anguished time is neither unprecedented nor without purpose. Mother Teresa wrote of such a time in personal letters that were later compiled in the book, <u>Mother Teresa, Come Be My Light</u>.[19] There is evidence in Paul's letters that he experienced the silence of God in his prayers (2 Corinthians 12:8). John of the Cross, a 16th century Spanish monk and mystic, wrote of "The Dark Night of the Soul." He taught that such times are not a punishment but a period of spiritual discipline leading to greater revelation. When the psalmist writes of the *"regions dark and deep"* (v. 6) and asks, *"Why do you cast my soul away?"* (v. 14), he is voicing something similar to a "dark night of the soul." According to John of the Cross, this difficult but holy time teaches humility, spiritual meekness, increased spiritual focus, and obedience.[20] Almost always a deepened understanding of God is being formed. Rather than death, it is the beginning of life. Rather than the darkness of the coffin, perhaps it is the darkness of a womb. But while we wait, we ask the hard questions.

Jesus also waited in the dark. He stated on that fretful night, in the Garden of Gethsemane, *"My soul is overwhelmed with sorrow to the point of death"* (Mark 14:34, NIV). Three times he prayed, and three times there was no answer. He waited on the cross. Mockers shouted, *"He trusts in God; let God deliver him now, if he desires him"* (Matthew 27:43). Would God answer now? Could God save him now? Silence. *"My God, my God, why have you forsaken me?"* (Matthew 27:46; Psalm 22:1). In his complete obedience, with no tangible evidence or physical sense that anything but darkness and death awaited, Jesus submitted himself completely to God's will.

Then darkness came over the whole land as Jesus bore the sins of the world upon his shoulders and felt the separation from the presence of God. *"Your wrath lies heavy upon me, and you overwhelm me"* (v. 7). Three more days he waited in the grave. *"You have put me in the depths of the pit... shut in so that I cannot escape"* (v. 6, 8). Then, sometime in the darkness before the dawn, God acted.

Does God work wonders for the dead? Is his steadfast love declared from the grave? God has answered our direct and honest questions. In Jesus, the answer is a resounding, "Yes!" God acted in power and glory when he raised Jesus from the dead, thereby enabling every believer the same new, glorious life (Ephesians 1:19–20). Because Jesus waited in the darkness, we are never separated from God and his love (Romans 8:35–39). Though the night is long, we are not alone. Jesus, our bright morning star, has risen in our hearts and shines in the darkness (2 Peter 1:19). Praise be to God who raises us up from the grave.

REFLECTION:

What relationship in your life has required that you wait before you knew the outcome? What did (does) it require of you while you wait?

DAY 21

YOU WHO FORGET GOD

Read Psalm 50.
Psalm after psalm, we have heard the persistent complaint against God's silence. The psalmist seeks God's attention, convinced that God will call to account the unrighteous. Finally, in Psalm 50, God condescends to speak, not just to the psalmist but to the heavens and the earth (v. 1, 4). With his speech, he brings forth judgment for both the righteous and the wicked. To both his people and those not his people he says, "I rebuke you," and he lays the charges at their feet. Both parties have forgotten the Mighty One, God the Lord, perfection and beauty, surrounded by fire and tempest, the one able to summon the heavens and the earth (v. 1–4). They forgot he was the judge of all people.

Perhaps God kept his silence too long. The people took the beauty of a sacrificial life—the awe and wonder of worship, the outpouring of the whole self as an offering to God (Romans 12:1)—and directed it towards themselves. Relationship turned into religion. Reverence for God gave way to reverence for worship and a certain self-importance. Extravagant robes were made for the educated and erudite. Processionals and fanfare were formed for distinguished persons of authority. The sensual pleasures of incense and oil anointed them as holy. Praise and admiration filled the rafters for those able to give much. The whole spectacle became about themselves. Their sacrifices were empty and meaningless (v. 8–13). It was all a hypocrisy, not to mention deceitful and disrespectful to the One they used in the process. They neglected their vows (v. 14), believing the blessing of God could be bought with rote actions and phrases, with sacrifices that cost them nothing more than cold, hard cash (2 Samuel 24:24). They had forgotten why God called them in the first place. This happens to religious people sometimes. Perhaps it is the reason for the silence.

For the wicked, God also kept his silence. They mistook God's silence for weakness. They mistook his patience for powerlessness. With no imminent judgment or threat, they reviled discipline and rejected God's word (v. 17), kept company with thieves and adulterers (v. 18), and spoke evil and deceit, slandering their own brothers and mothers (v. 19–20). They worshiped idols, making gods that looked like themselves—cheaply painted celebrities, ravenous corporate barons, power-hungry rich, and the pitiful powerbrokers who sell their souls down the river (v. 21). By every measure, the wicked disregarded and disrespected God. They acted as if he and his beautiful, creative moral universe were a figment of the imagination. For them, his silence was a measure of the utmost mercy. Here is what God speaks to both the righteous and the unrighteous:

> *"Mark this, then, you who forget God,*
> *lest I tear you apart, and there be none to deliver!"*
>
> **PSALM 50:22**

It is both a warning and a promise, a judgment and a mercy. For the wicked, they have forgotten the God who can break the cedars, shake the wilderness, and strip the forest bare, who thunders over the water (Psalm 29). They forgot the God who can rip them apart with a blast from his nostrils (Psalm 18:15). He is holy, powerful, righteous, and just. Only by his silence has he spared them, and only for the time being. Only for a time.

> *"The Lord is not slow to fulfill his promise as some count slowness, but is patient toward you, not wishing that any should perish, but that all should reach repentance. But the day of the Lord will come like a thief, and then the heavens will pass away with a roar, and the heavenly bodies will be burned up and dissolved, and the earth and the works that are done on it will be exposed."*
>
> **2 PETER 3:9–10**

For the righteous, ironic designation that it is, they too have forgotten that they are subject to the same judgment that will cover the earth and the heavens in God's perfect timing. No one will escape God's purifying truth when it comes (Hebrews 4:13; 2 Thessalonians 1:5–10). They have forgotten that the covenant they made with God is not a free pass to continue their selfish ways (Romans 6:1–2). It is not a token to evade judgment. It is an invitation to be transformed by it. It is a gateway to be made new. It burns like a fire through the dross of our lives, leaving only what is precious, pure, and holy (1 Corinthians 3:12–15). It comes to us through God's Word (Hebrews 4:12), through his Spirit (John 16:8–11), and through the Son (John 5:27). It is a gift, and in the end, it is a mercy. If we ignore these gifts from God, not only will we forget him, but we will not recognize him when we see him (Matthew 25:31–46). And Jesus will say on that final day, *"I never knew you"* (Matthew 7:21–23).

Because the final day has not yet come, there is still an element of mercy woven into the final verse. To both groups, the word of the Lord says to offer a sacrifice of thanksgiving (v. 14, 23). These fellowship or peace offerings were offered in thanks to God by those who had been delivered from great peril.

As if to remind them that he could have annihilated them, God instructs them to thank him for sparing their lives and to make peace (Leviticus 7:12–15). Then they shall order their ways rightly, according to God's Word. Despite the definitive nature of judgment in Psalm 50, the door on the subject has not yet closed. It has been left open just long enough, leaving room for Someone to deliver.

> *"Wait for his Son from heaven, whom he raised from the dead, Jesus who delivers us from the wrath to come."*
>
> **1 THESSALONIANS 1:10**

> *"Those who were not my people I will call 'my people,' and her who was not beloved I will call 'beloved.'"*
> *"And in the very place where it was said to them, 'You are not my people,' there they will be called 'sons of the living God.'"*
>
> **ROMANS 9:25–26**

REFLECTION:

Do you believe God is at work for the salvation of those who do not yet know him? Can you think of a person who was an antagonist to God but is now a faithful follower of Christ? What happened, in your opinion?

NOTES

WEEK 4

PSALMS OF

INTERNAL LAMENT

Introduction to the Psalms of Internal Lament

As we continue in our study of the Psalms of Lament, we discover that the enemy has once again shifted. The inflicted suffering no longer comes from an outside attack or from God, but from the psalmist's own sinful behavior. The well-being God designed us for has been frustrated by sin. The difficult dialogues have subsided, and guilt is conceded. The psalmist discovers, however, that the fullness of life is not achieved by "not sinning" but by living in God's merciful and gracious forgiveness. These psalms are excellent examples of prayers of confession and complete trust in God's merciful nature. In these psalms, we deepen our understanding of God's nature to forgive, which comes from his righteousness, never our own. We see the structure of his plan of salvation, where forgiveness comes through God's righteousness, most perfectly seen in Jesus on the cross, who covers all our sins.

DAY 22

MAN IN HIS POMP

Read Psalm 49.

"In this world nothing can be said to be certain, except death and taxes." Ben Franklin wrote this famous phrase in a letter, but Psalm 49 captured its essence thousands of years before. Struggling to understand the disparity between rich and poor, the psalmist boils down humanity's existence to two essential elements: money and death. Certainly, there has always been an element of society that ruled over another. The psalmist calls its representative the *"man in his pomp"* (v. 12). We might call him "the big dog" or "The Man." This person rules in power at the expense of others. But another category of society—the poor and lowly—feels constantly in debt to the *"man in his pomp."* Rent, overdraft fees, interest payments, layaway charges—such is their life. The psalmist's aim is not to determine why this distinction exists but to dispel its power.

The *"man in his pomp"* is not a statement about wealth but attitude. The psalm reveals the characteristics of the foolish man: he cheats (v. 5), boasts (v. 6), increases his glory (v. 16, 17), and counts himself blessed (v. 18) on his own accomplishments (v. 6). He has everything going for him: an extravagant home (v. 16), a lineage of land titles (v. 11), and social approval (v. 13, 18). He spends his lifetime acquiring such things, only to leave it all to others (v. 10). The psalmist calls it *"foolish confidence"* (v. 13) to trust the transitory material blessings of this life and ignore (*"without understanding"*) that the blessing is short-lived. It is easy to envy a person whose life seems so full of ease, comfort, pleasure, and approval. But the psalmist insists that there is no distinction between the rich or poor, the highborn or the lowly. In the end, each goes down to the grave.

Everyone knows the adage, "You can't take it with you when you go." The psalmist expands on the idea. Even if one could take their wealth to the grave, perhaps like Egyptian kings who stored their treasure in their tombs, what good would it serve? Could it buy their life back, to *"live on forever and never see the pit"* (v. 9)? Consider this: No man paid off God to earn his place in the world, high or low. God determined the exact time and place of man's entry. No man can bribe God regarding the terms of his exit either—to delay or expedite it. Before God, all men are equal in status. But even if one could make a deal with God to extend life indefinitely, even eternally, what would the cost be? Who sets the terms? The psalmist is clear: Eternal life comes at a price too high for anyone to pay, even *"man in his pomp."*

So, we have addressed one of Ben Franklin's maxims—death is certain. Now we find ourselves on the doorstep of the other—a tax of sorts, a ransom, a costly price to be paid. Verse 7 has created an enigma, though. The deal itself is not impossible—but the price is. What is the most a man could pay to buy his life from God, if he could? The answer would not be gold, silver, stocks, or land deeds. God already owns all the riches of the world. It would be his own life, his own blood. The most a man could give would be his very life. Yet his life is already spent. Man can only come as a borrower to God, who is the lender. Man's offer would be like buying a new car with a loan based on the collateral of an old, beat-up jalopy. Man's bargain would be like trying to buy a house based on the sale of that exact same house. The transaction would negate itself. It is a simple but callous fact that our life does not have sufficient trade-in value for eternal life. If we want to understand anything about life after death, we must realize that God sets the terms.

The eternal God, Creator of the universe, has given everything to us. He gave us the light of the sun and moon, a time to work and a time to rest. He provided plants and animals, food and materials, nourishment and shelter. He gave us life, selected our DNA, orchestrated our talents, and designed our physical characteristics. He inspired us with ideas and knowledge to work and prosper. He surrounds us with people for help, support, love, and friendship. We are a part of his creation, and we are his. If when we die, we wish to purchase our life from him, what would be the sum of our lives? They are priceless. We are debtors, all of us—rich and poor, highborn or lowly. We owe God our lives.

God understood that we could never pay the cost. And yet, unwilling to consign us to a life of hopelessness, doomed to the grave, he made a ransom for us. Jesus, God made flesh, the only one found worthy and acceptable (Revelation 5:9), paid the costly price (v. 8) of his life slain on the cross, so that we would live free from the power of death (v. 15). This is the certainty we have through Jesus Christ: though we die, yet shall we live (John 11:25). What shall we give to one who has cancelled our debt and set us free?

REFLECTION:

The psalmist does not give a detailed description of the poor and lowly, yet it is clear he considers himself in that camp. According to Matthew 5:3–11, how did Jesus define this group? How are they different than the "man of pomp" in Psalm 49?

DAY 23

MERCY WITHOUT MERIT

Read Psalm 143.
In our previous section of the Psalms of Lament, we became familiar with the psalmist's plea for judgment, primarily of the enemy. However, in Psalm 143, we hear David's plea for God *not* to judge, for he knows "*no one living is righteous*" before God (v. 2). Indeed, he seems less concerned with the outside enemy than with his own position before God. In this beautiful petition for mercy, David unveils God's character in a new way and helps us establish the proper posture before him.

David opens the psalm with an appeal for mercy. In the characteristic language of many of his psalms, David begins by acclaiming God's attributes. It is these qualities that David will call upon for mercy. He asserts that only God is righteous (v. 1–2), and only God's righteousness can save him (v. 11). Before he prays, David sets his heart on God's character. This is an effective model for all prayer. First, we properly ascribe authority and power to God. Then we can better align our requests with his nature. In this prayer, David could have focused on his enemy's faults. But because David begins with God's character of righteousness and faithfulness, the Spirit leads the psalmist to understand his real need: mercy for himself.

God's righteousness is our standard. This criterion has been established throughout the psalms, and David is quick to recognize that he cannot meet the standard. "*No one living is righteous before you*" (v. 2). As he considers the work of his hands, no doubt in response to his enemy, his heart is "appalled" (v. 4). We feel this way too, sometimes. David's soul is in a dark place and his spirit is faint (v. 3). Recognizing his own weakness and inadequacy to redeem himself, he calls to God, who alone can help. Nowhere in this psalm do we see David rely on his own self-sufficiency or merit to address his own sins. His posture before God is one of humility and submission (v. 6, 7, 10), completely yielded to God. It is not a position of debasement, but of trust and confidence in God's love for him. "*I stretch out my hands… Teach me… Let me hear in the morning of your steadfast love*" (v. 6, 8, 10). What a beautiful prayer to offer to the Lord as the basis of our need for his mercy!

We are like David, appalled at the condition of our own hearts. We understand our need for mercy because we can glimpse elements of God's righteousness. His goodness compels us towards him, towards a righteousness in ourselves that is sometimes just out of reach. We know our need for forgiveness. We know our sins and our weaknesses. But still we find ourselves wrapped up in the steadfast love of God (v. 8, 12), not afraid, but yearning for more (v. 6). God's mercy, his propensity to forgive and renew us, comes from his abundant righteousness and faithfulness.

David understood that it was not his own righteousness that counted, but God's. The Spirit had given David wisdom to see God's great plan of salvation before it was fully enacted. God's righteousness came to earth in the form of his Son, Jesus. Jesus exhibited God's righteousness while he lived and walked on the earth. Then, according to God's plan, that righteousness bore our sins on the cross in order that we might be forgiven of our appalling burden. Jesus's sacrifice is the greatest act of mercy ever committed.

By his mercy, God helps us when our spirits are faint (v. 4, 9). The soul that is parched from trying to earn approval is refreshed by Jesus's love (v. 6, 8). Jesus is the refuge from the voice of the Accuser who says that we are never good enough (v. 3, 9). Jesus fills us and gives us what we need most (2 Corinthians 12:9–10). He provides eternal rest for our souls (Hebrews 4:1–11). Like David, let us be quick to yield ourselves to his mercies, humbling ourselves before him in confidence of his love that awakens us each day to begin again.

> *"But this I call to mind,*
> *and therefore I have hope:*
> *The steadfast love of the LORD never ceases;*
> *his mercies never come to an end;*
> *they are new every morning;*
> *great is your faithfulness."*
>
> **LAMENTATIONS 3:21–23**

> *"And when Jesus heard it, he said to them,*
> *'Those who are well have no need of a physician, but those who are sick. I came not to call the righteous, but sinners.'"*
>
> **MARK 2:17**

REFLECTION:

Do you ever feel tired or exhausted from your efforts to be good enough?

Is there something you are still doing to try to earn God's favor? Explain.

According to 2 Corinthians 12:9–10, what is the blessing (and mercy) that comes from letting Jesus be our righteousness?

DAY 24

AGAINST YOU ONLY HAVE I SINNED

Read Psalm 51.
In Psalm 51, we eavesdrop on a man's personal confession before God. David is distraught and feels separated from the joyful, exuberant presence of God. David's sins were many and various, but this psalm has a specific history. Psalm 51 was written in response to David's adulterous affair with Bathsheba, recounted in 2 Samuel 11–12. There unfolds the scandalous story of the king's lust and extramarital relationship. A pregnancy ensues along with a plot to deceive Bathsheba's husband, Uriah. Finally, David orders Uriah to the front line of the military battle and orchestrates his murder through a strategic retreat. This is the sin that troubles David's soul in Psalm 51.

Like Psalm 143, David begins with a plea for mercy based on God's core characteristic—his steadfast love. He dares not approach God on any other basis than God's covenantal love for him. But he is quick to get to his part in the transaction. While he does not name his particular offenses, we can make an intimidating list based on the 2 Samuel passage. Lust, adultery, deceit, envy, and murder top the list. All of these are an affront to God's law, and no less than four of the Ten Commandments have been broken. To David's credit, he makes no argument against his guilt and takes ownership of his actions. He concedes that they are "*my transgressions… my iniquity… my sins*" (v. 1–2). In verse 3 he says, "*For I know my transgressions and my sin is ever before me.*" Sin is personal, and it clings to us like a foul stench soaked into the threads of our fabric. It stinks with every movement and fills us with disgust.

Unfortunately, sin damages more than our conscience. Often, the great tragedy of sin is not the actual transgression, but the repercussions of it. Sin is progressive. We justify a sin as small or secretive, thinking it impacts no one but ourselves. But sin always expands in rippling circles, affecting others. This was true for David. It was just a look—but it resulted in murder. In its wake, it brought tragedy to Bathsheba, who lost both her husband and the conceived child. It brought pain and suffering to Uriah's family. It drew the military leaders into the sinful plot, and a retinue of soldiers were pointlessly slaughtered. It tarnished the king's reputation and dragged him into deep, soulful depression. The result of sin is death, in many ways, on many levels. Such explains why the God of life and love is so gravely wounded by our seemingly obscure and innocuous sin.

David knows his sins because he knows his God. He completely understands that it is God whom he has most grievously offended. He speaks rightly in verse 4, "*Against you, you only, have I sinned and done what is evil in your sight.*" David understood that there was a law that governed the created world, infused with the love and righteousness of God. This moral law was further developed in the written and spoken law, the Torah. It was the pattern of how to live in the kingdom and reflected the character of God himself. David understood that by breaking the law he had offended the very nature of God, which was the basis of the law itself. The only resolution would come with God's judgment.

At its best, sin means to "miss the mark," to fail to meet God's standard for living. At its worst, sin is a blatant revolt against God (Romans 8:7). Psalm 143:2 reminds us that there is no one living who is righteous before God. All have turned aside from the mark and have become corrupt (Psalm 14:3). Sin is not only progressive, but it is pervasive. None of us escape its stain. As David says, it is inbred in us. It is in our nature to sin (v. 5). In that sense, sin has hit its target.

We often think our sin is private, that no one needs to know. We think we can make amends for our offenses. But we cannot hide or cover our sins. God, who is sovereign and omniscient, still knows our sins (Psalm 139:1–3, 23–24). And one day every sin will be made known, one way or another (Luke 8:17). Every egregious act has been registered in God's moral universe. Every sin is out there; all are known.

Unconfessed, the sin will attach itself to us like a virus, invading our hearts, our memories, and our imaginations. It will infect and warp our reality. We pretend that we do not feel its rancid effect, wrenching our stomachs and our souls. Day after day, night after night, we will convince ourselves that we are strong, and that time will abate the damage it is wreaking on us. But it never does. Finally, in one of our night sweats, weak but filled with a strange lucidity, the fever will break, and we will beg God for his mercy. It will all come up, gladly, to expose it to God's judgment. We will be happy to be done with it.

> *"Have mercy on me, O God,*
> *according to your steadfast love;*
> *according to your abundant mercy*
> *blot out my transgressions.*
> *Wash me thoroughly from my iniquity,*
> *and cleanse me from my sin!"*

PSALM 51:1–2

REFLECTION:

Reflect upon one of your small, quiet (maybe not so quiet?) rebellions against God.

In what ways does it hurt God?

In what ways does it hurt others?

In what ways does it hurt you?

DAY 25

THE HEAVY GRACE OF GUILT

Read Psalm 38.
Guilt is a strange gift of grace, as unwelcome as heartburn or headaches. Recognized in our sleepless nights, high blood pressure, anxiety, or depression—a guilty conscience is the outward and visible sign of an inward and spiritual truth.[21] Guilt is an exasperating sacrament, of sorts, that accompanies our sin. In Psalm 38, David experiences the double-edged nature of his guilt, in both body and spirit. Like us, he grieves not only the pain he has brought upon himself, but also God's rebuke and waning presence in his life. It is a two-sided pressure that is too much to bear for his Spirit-made constitution. Thankfully, in this guttural exposé on guilt, this prayer for relief, we find the remedy for our pain comes from its source. Our help is very near.

Psalm 38 teaches us that our physical actions impact our spirit, and our spiritual actions impact our body. In God's well-ordered universe, the two are always intertwined. When we sin physically—when we cheat, steal, or lie—our spirits are wounded. We feel shame, self-hate, fear, hopelessness, or worry. When we sin spiritually—in unforgiveness, hatred, envy, or criticism—our bodies suffer in physical ways. Psalm 38 describes the symptoms. The effects may not be immediate, but they happen over time. David makes this connection in verse 3: "*There is no soundness in my flesh because of your indignation, there is no health in my bones because of my sin.*" To understand the effect of sin on ourselves and in the world, we must see this connection. God designed mankind—flesh, bones, sinews, joints, and blood—to be in sync with his Spirit. In the beginning, he breathed his Spirit into our material form, and we thrive in that holy combination (Genesis 2:7; Psalm 104:29–30). Guilt reveals that there is something out of joint with that relationship. There is a disconnect. It hurts to be out of sync with God.

David is besieged by the weight of his sins in a variety of physical ways: depression (v. 6), achiness (v. 7), lethargy (v. 10), and distraction (v. 13). There are other material implications too. In verse 11, his friends and family stand aloof. Either embarrassed for him or at a loss of what to say, they leave him alone in his anguish. His adversaries, on the other hand, draw near. Sensing weakness, they plot to take advantage of his debilitated state (v. 12, 19). There is no soundness in his flesh.

But David's body is the least of his worries. He feels the weight of his wounded spirit. God's rebuke feels like "arrows" burrowing in his skin, and he feels the heavy pressure of God's hand (v. 2). He longs for the connection that strengthened him and lit up his eyes (v. 9–10), but it has gone from him. Unconfessed sin has spiritual ramifications.

Guilt is a work of the Spirit in our bodies—God's not-so-subtle attempt to get our attention. David was anointed in the Spirit long before the Holy Spirit was poured out on the Day of Pentecost (1 Samuel 16:13). As Christians, we know that our bodies are filled with the living Spirit. Paul teaches us that our bodies are the "*the temple of the Holy Spirit, who is in [us], whom [we] have received from God*" (1 Corinthians 6:19 NIV). Guilt happens in response to the Spirit's presence, not in its absence. Can we suffer as David describes without a strong understanding of God's presence? Yet, we can grieve the Holy Spirit (Ephesians 4:30). We risk the greatest casualty of its quiet retreat, which we provoke as we disregard its voice (Isaiah 59:2). Guilt is the clamor of the Spirit to get our attention. Like a wounded cat that wails in the night, God's Spirit is relentless to draw our attention to the injury.

The unbearable weight that David experiences is a mercy, for it means the Spirit is still at work in him—and in us too. "*For your arrows have sunk into me, and your hand has come down on me*" (v. 2). Though it sounds like daggers meant to wound David, perhaps it is really the hook with which God reels David back to shore or the hand that draws him out of the deep. The Spirit of Truth is faithful to act in our hearts, convicting us of our sins, pricking us where we need it (John 16:8; 1 Thessalonians 1:5). The conviction of the Spirit never condemns us but draws us back to Jesus (John 14:26) and brings us to a new life of peace, renewed in the Spirit (Romans 8:1–2).

It is hard for us to kick against the goads (Acts 26:14). We resist the heavy hand of the Spirit as if we can eradicate its impact. We writhe in our guilt, inside and out, until we collapse in exhaustion under the weight. Then finally, when we are stilled, too weak to resist our persistent and faithful God, we let him have his way. His arrows have sunk in. His strong hand is upon us, and he picks us up off the floor. His hand is strong, but his rebuke is gentle. His wrath was spent on Christ Jesus. Our help is very near (v. 21).

REFLECTION:

Can you recall a time when a guilty conscience weighed heavily upon you? How did you respond? Did you see God working in it for good?

DAY 26

THE TRUTH ABOUT CONFESSION

Read Psalm 51.
It is hard to speak the truth about ourselves. We have an embellished image in our minds that is sometimes only slightly hinged to reality. Why are we surprised when we sin? Do we know ourselves so little? We are shocked to find out that we are weak, arrogant, foolish, and selfish. It hurts to be honest with ourselves. But if we are ever to have an authentic relationship, it must begin in truth—based on who we really are. How much more so with God. In Psalm 51, David models the sweet and trusting movement from confession to freedom, from truth to joy.

After an appeal for mercy, David begins his confession. 2 Samuel 12 relays the conversation in David's mind and heart. He knows that the Lord delights in truth (v. 6) and so do we. Jesus said, *"the truth will set you free"* (John 8:32), and we find the relief is palpable. In our shame, we form a shell around ourselves to protect our image—a shiny, pearlized finish. Inside our dank cell, we remain dark and amorphous, trapped by the fear that we will be known as we are. Still God calls us into the light. He calls us to trust him, trust in his mercy, and trust in his power to change us. He is making something new and beautiful. Our confession makes us open, vulnerable, and real. It breaks the shell of our shame and begins an open dialogue with God. Confession is the beginning of freedom.

What shall we say? We hardly know. We hesitate. We fumble with our words. But our effort is bolstered by the strength of the Holy Spirit. As we speak, he draws near (James 4:8). The Spirit leads us in truth (John 16:13) and prompts us to honest penitence before God. Perhaps this is what David means in verse 6, *"you teach me wisdom in the secret heart."* With the Spirit as a guide, we discover thoughts and attitudes that we did not at first recognize as sinful or hurtful. God's Word helps us identify specific actions that need confession (Hebrews 4:12–13). Liturgies focused on confession help us recall our offenses against God. Writing our sins in a journal and saying them aloud help us to see and voice our culpability. These exercises help bring what is hidden to the light. We need not worry. We are not alone. Jesus himself, our High Priest and Mediator, escorts us to the throne of grace (Hebrews 4:16). In God's remarkable love and mercy, he ushers us back to himself through something as simple as agreeing with him about who we are and who we are meant to be.

Like David in Psalm 38, our bodies and spirits can no longer bear the weight of our sins and their consequences. Like the psalmist in Psalm 49, we cannot pay the price for our own sin. We concede that our problem is God's problem. This is another truth-telling. We cannot fix the problem of sin on our own. But we are not meant to. First John 1:8–9 says, *"If we say we have no sin, we deceive ourselves and the truth is not in us. If we confess our sins, he is faithful and just to forgive us our sins and to cleanse us from all unrighteousness."* Immediately. In the account of 2 Samuel 12:13, David's confession and forgiveness happen in the same verse. We see the same movement in verses 6, 7, and 8. There is no space, no gap, no time lapse, no additional penitential action. It is done. The price was paid on our behalf when Jesus bore our sins on the cross. We must speak this truth to ourselves again and again. We must let Jesus speak it over us. "*It is finished*" (John 19:30). Our joy is built upon that truth.

When we confess our sins to God in the name of Jesus, we are quickly ushered into the reality of his kingdom. We see the truth from God's perspective. Confession is not just telling the truth about ourselves but also about God. We are weak, but he is strong. We are sorry, but he is forgiving. We are wrong, but he is right. We hurt others, but he is the healer. We need help. He is willing and able. We need love. He loves us. In his presence we see the truth, and we hear him speak the truth over us. Satan tells us that we are worthless, but Jesus proved that we are of inestimable value (Matthew 13:45–46). The accuser tells us that we will never change, but our Father in heaven promises that he is making us new (2 Corinthians 5:17; Revelation 21:5). The enemy tells us that our past defines us, but Jesus reveals his glorious plan for us (John 17:22, 24; Romans 8:18). As we humble ourselves before the Lord, it is not the truth we offer, but the truth he speaks over us that becomes our new life.

Suddenly we are renewed in the Spirit (v. 10), and instantly we feel the rush of our new heart beating (Ezekiel 36:26). We are no longer ashamed, hiding in our shell. We step with freedom into God's kingdom in delight, wisdom, joy, gladness, righteousness, salvation, and praise (v. 6–15). In faith, we have trusted God enough to tell the truth about ourselves. In turn, he is making us true. We are no longer covered by a false facade, but authentic to the core, in perfect line with who he has made us to be. "*O Lord, open my lips, and my mouth will declare your praise*" (v. 15).

REFLECTION:

Consider using this space to write your confession to God. You may want to try using the pattern "I am _____, but you, Lord are _____." As you prepare, ask God to speak his truth in your heart.

DAY 27

THE FRIENDSHIP OF GOD

Read Psalm 25.
There is something wonderfully fresh and expectant about this psalm of lament. Like sunlight peering from behind a heavy cloud, hope rises over the darkness of David's sin and guilt. Though David is still pleading for God's mercy, we see his eagerness to rejoin God's covenantal friendship. Psalm 25 is a beautiful psalm of repentance and reconciliation, a pivotal turn towards God. David prays once again based on his understanding of God's character, nature, and loving commitment. Psalm 25 draws us into God's reciprocal movement, and we discover that we, too, are called friends of God.

Like two friends who have come through a difficult conversation, David comes to God at a crossroads. How will it be after his transgression, after the broken trust? David prays, optimistically confident in God's mercy and faithfulness. Repentance is a hopeful act. The Lord is open, ready to listen. A reconciliation is at hand. The two must reestablish what it means to be in covenantal relationship. Both friends must turn towards each other.

David yearns to walk together again with God. "*Make me to know your ways, O LORD; teach me your paths*" (v. 4). "*He leads the humble in what is right, and teaches the humble his way. All the paths of the LORD are steadfast love and faithfulness*" (v. 9–10). David promises to turn his life back to the pattern God has set according to his Word. This is how it is with friends, even friends who have been at odds. We agree to continue our walk together. The value of the friendship is worth the effort to restore trust and affection. Jesus said, "*If you obey my commands, you will remain in my love…You are my friends, if you do what I command.*" (John 15:10, 14 NIV). If we want to walk with Jesus, we must recommit ourselves to his commands. To engage deeply and intimately with the Lord Jesus, we must walk where he walks. As Amos said, "*Do two walk together, unless they have agreed to meet?*" (Amos 3:3). So we have the beginning of a restored relationship, an agreement to walk together in the same direction.

Reconciliation is based on how we choose to remember. David makes an interesting plea that demands a conscious and complex memory. "*Remember your mercy, O LORD, and your steadfast love… Remember not the sins of my youth or my transgressions*" (v. 6–7). David's request is based squarely upon God's merciful and unchangeable nature. Throughout Scripture, God attests that he forgets the sins of his people when they turn to him. "*I will remember their sin no more*" (Jeremiah 31:34). But he remembers to show mercy, compassion, love, and forgiveness for generations (Exodus 34:7). So, David calls upon this biased memory to, once again, remember mercy but forget sins.[22] That is how it is with those we love. We must have a fluid, failing memory in some things—the hurts and pains we let go. But we retain an unfaltering memory of our love and commitment, never letting go. We must turn our minds to the essential foundations of our relationship, which in the end is always love.

In the confidence of God's steadfast love, David utters the heart of his prayer. "*Remember me*" (v. 7). "*Turn to me*" (v. 16). He reminds God of their friendship and the remarkable covenant made to him, an everlasting dynasty under his name (v. 14). God fulfilled this promise in Jesus, and it is only through Jesus that God can be called our friend (Matthew 1:1–17). Jesus said, "*Greater love has no one than this, that someone lay down his life for his friends. You are my friends*" (John 15:13–14). God turned to David and remembered his promise, though he had a much greater plan than David would ever conceive. His friendship and covenant would extend to all who desired it, rich or poor, religious or irreligious, sorrowful and repentant—every person who wanted to turn to the Lord, for no good reason except that God turned toward them (Isaiah 55:3–7).

Here is the amazing friendship of God, that while we were still sinners, God made a way for us to be restored to divine favor with him (Romans 5:8). In his biased love for us, he remembered us—that we are made of dust (Psalm 103:13–14). In compassion, he made his Son to be our reconciliation, even though we had nothing more to offer except our feeble efforts to try again and our desire to still be called his own. That is how it is with friends.

> "*Now that we are set right with God by means of this sacrificial death, the consummate blood sacrifice, there is no longer a question of being at odds with God in any way. If, when we were at our worst, we were put on friendly terms with God by the sacrificial death of his Son, now that we're at our best, just think of how our lives will expand and deepen by means of his resurrection life! Now that we have actually received this amazing friendship with God, we are no longer content to simply say it in plodding prose. We sing and shout our praises to God through Jesus, the Messiah!*"
>
> **ROMANS 5:9–11, MSG**

Let us turn now to our friend and accept his ever-ready offer of reconciliation.

REFLECTION:

What do you desire most from the friendship of God? Receive it through Jesus, your friend (John 16:23).

DAY 28

OUT OF THE DEPTHS

Read Psalm 130.
Psalm 130 offers a refrain that has been an anthem of hope throughout the ages. "*I wait for the LORD, my soul waits... more than watchmen for the morning*" (v. 4–5). In its simplicity, this psalm encompasses the great expanse between our depths of suffering and God's merciful redemption. It forms a continuum upon which we all move, between the despair of our very worst days and the confidence that God has promised us more. While Psalm 130 is still very much a lament, it beautifully lays the foundation for the Gospel and a clear reason to cling to hope.

The psalmist speaks of a depth unknown. We do not know the psalmist's name, or the context of his situation, but familiar terms of lament, "*the pit,*" "*the darkness,*" and "*the grave,*" show us that his circumstances are dire. He cries out from "*the depths,*" a term every person has experienced in some degree at some time, to presumably the heights of the heavens (Psalm 148:1). The psalmist trusts that his plea will be heard, for God is everywhere (Psalm 8:1), and everywhere he hears our cries (Exodus 3:7–8). For the one who made the ear promised, "*Before they call, I will answer; while they are still speaking, I will hear*" (Isaiah 65:24). David's cry (and ours) rings out throughout the universe to a God who promised he would hear.

The psalmist does not pray for relief from an assaulting army or vindication against an adversary. He does not decree justice for the wicked. He prays for mercy for himself. The basis for God to hear his cry is God's mercy and his propensity to forgive. The psalmist does not claim any merit of his own or make any case for himself (v. 3). He does not recite a recommitment to God's law or prostrate himself in prayer. He offers nothing. His cry is bold because it is founded on God's nature to lift up and redeem those who are lowly and broken and downcast (Psalm 113:5–9; 138:6). This is the heart of the Gospel for us. "*While we were still weak, at the right time Christ died for the ungodly.... God shows his love for us in that while we were still sinners, Christ died for us*" (Romans 5:6, 8). God acts in mercy towards us, through no merit of our own, before we ask.

This transaction is the basis for every new beginning, every new start. We can call it forgiveness, as the psalmist does. For it is surely that. But it is also redemption. It is also steadfast love (v. 4, 7). It is the way of God, through Christ, for everyone who finds themselves in the depths. It is the basis of new life. It ushers the power and love of Christ into every situation. Nothing can be the same again, not even the depths.

Christ has transformed our depths. Though our situation may not have materially changed (yet), we can wait with hope. We wait for the God who raises everything up (Luke 7:22), who sets boundaries on death (1 Corinthians 15:54–55; Revelation 21:4), on suffering (1 Peter 5:10), and on sin (Romans 6:6–7; 8:2). We wait for the God who proved his love by entering our suffering and going down to the depths, so that the depths are never the end of our story. We wait with hope for the God who said he will return in victory to restore and make all things new.

While we wait, we can try to grasp how deep is the love of Christ (Ephesians 3:18). To understand that is to understand our depths are no longer deep (Psalm 139:7–12). The distance between the depths and the heights has been eliminated. He is here. There is no distance between us. So, we wait as watchmen do for the sun to rise—confident, expectant, hopeful. Jesus is here, and with him is plentiful redemption.

REFLECTION:

Webster's Dictionary defines the word "redeem" as follows:

1. to buy back: repurchase, to get or win back,
2. to free from what distresses or harms, to free from captivity by payment of ransom, to extricate from or help overcome something detrimental, to release from blame or debt, to free from the consequences of sin
3. to change for the better, to reform
4. to repair, restore
5. to free from a lien by payment of an amount secured, to remove the obligation of payment, to convert into something of value, to make good, to fulfill.[23]

Which definition above appeals to you the most? How has God done this for you?

Write a prayer of praise to God for his steadfast love and mercy in all his ways with you.

NOTES

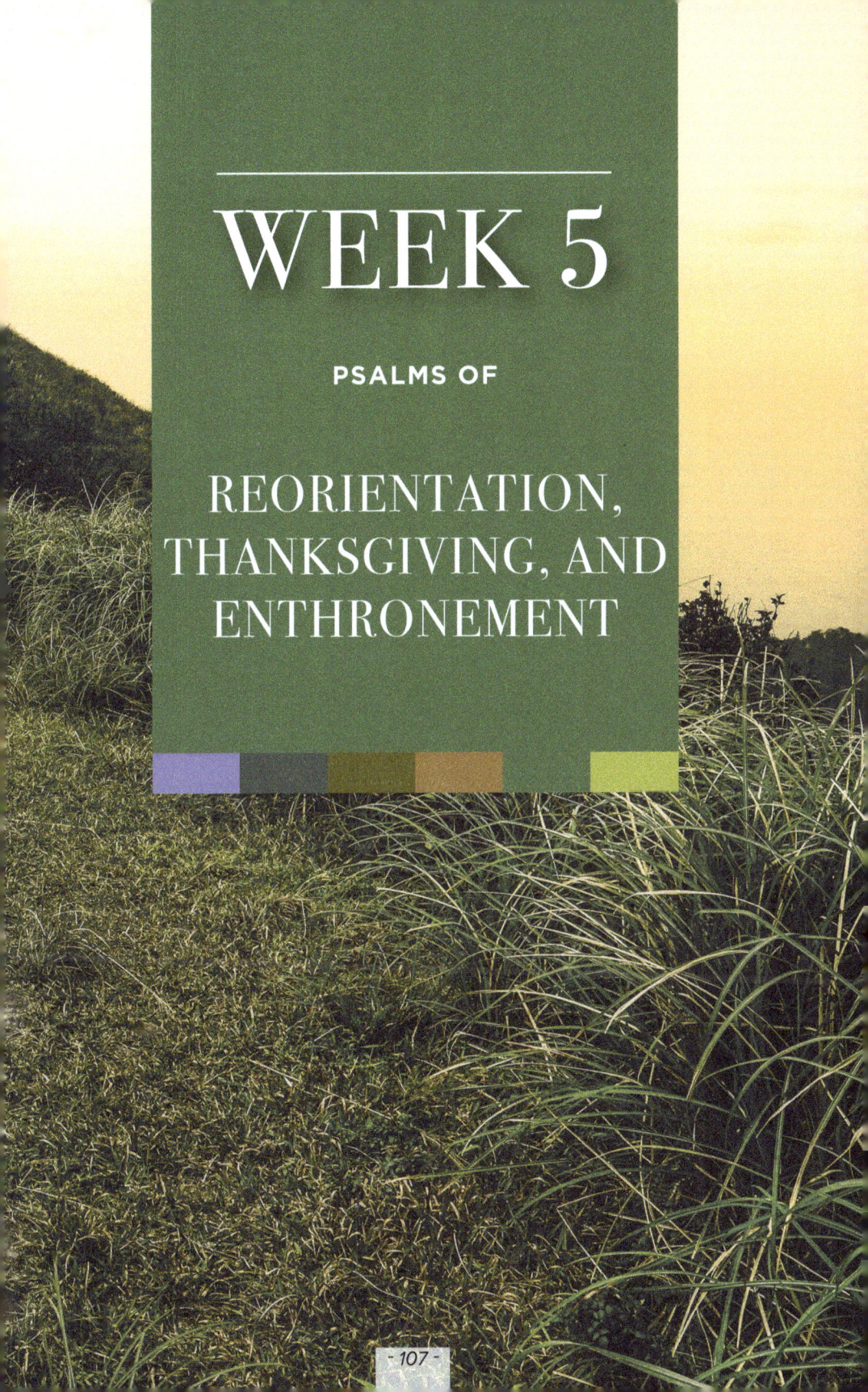

WEEK 5

PSALMS OF

REORIENTATION, THANKSGIVING, AND ENTHRONEMENT

Introduction to the Psalms of Reorientation, Thanksgiving and Enthronement

This lesson turns the corner from the Psalms of Lament. In Psalms 90 and 73, we discover a maturity and an understanding, as one having been through an ordeal with their faith still intact. The psalmist expresses a new tenacity in his relationship towards God. He conveys a deep understanding of God as sanctuary, refuge, and dwelling place. God himself is the reward.

In Psalms 30, 138, and 34, the psalmist acknowledges God's power and love to deliver him. The rescue is not one of natural outcomes, but specifically delivered through God's gracious and righteous hands. Such a shift in circumstances bends the knee in reverence, awe, and thanksgiving to God. The Thanksgiving Psalms teach us that, in God's kingdom, honor follows shame, joy follows sorrow, and life follows death. As Christians, we recognize this powerful, loving, and creative pattern in the death and resurrection of Jesus. The Thanksgiving Psalms set an example for the resurrected life in which we are to live.

In grateful response, we, along with the psalmist, learn to sing a "new song." God is making us a new creation. We discover that the song we sing is part of a festive coronation procession, where we put God on the throne in our lives. Psalms 96 and 99 are two Enthronement Psalms that speak of the coming of a new reign, a new kingdom. Justice, righteousness, and peace will be the foundation of this new government. Jesus regularly spoke of this kingdom and, indeed, ushered it in. These psalms teach us the spiritual discipline of celebration. Life in the new kingdom begins and ends with joy.

DAY 29

OUR REWARD AND OUR REALITY

Read Psalm 90.
In Psalm 90, we receive the blessing of wise counsel from a wise heart. Moses, the author of this psalm, is assessing the span of his life, the scope of his work, and the value of his mission on this afflicted earth. Perhaps he is gazing from Mt. Nebo, overlooking the promised land into which he will never cross (Deuteronomy 34:1). A clear sense of reality has come in his latter and departing days. With a mature perspective, he has reduced the meaning of life into a concise statement: the Lord is our dwelling place. This truth is the basis for understanding the meaning of our days on earth.

Moses understands God to be the one true reality in this world. God stands outside of time and space. Before the mountains were brought forth, God was God. His existence is eternal, and he is eternally present. "*From everlasting to everlasting*," from time immemorial, Moses says, "*You are*" (v. 2). Moses is perhaps remembering God's very name for himself, "*I AM WHO I AM*" in Exodus 3:14. Jesus made a similar statement, "*Before Abraham was, I am*" (John 8:58). He is present everywhere for all time. Furthermore, God's presence in our temporal world is dynamic and powerful. He is in control of every moment in the fleeting days and years that make up our fragile lives (v. 3–6). Everything about our lives is based on one sole understanding. God determines our reality. How we see our lives depends on how we see God.

In contrast to God's nature, Moses assesses the life of mankind. Man is dust that returns to dust (v. 3). The lifespan of any generation is short. Our lives, in comparison to God's eternity, are like the grass that withers and dies in a short cycle (v. 6). And within our brief subsistence, we toil under the trouble of each day (v. 10). In addition to our feeble condition, sin remains a thorn to us, causing us grief and invoking God's just wrath. The psalmist concludes that life is short, hard, broken, and ends pitiably in death. Not an optimistic outlook, from a mountaintop, reviewing the span of his days. But the psalmist does not end here. His circumstances, as material and definite as they may be, are not the basis of his reality.

Moses ends his psalm where he began it. In an appeal to God to give him a "*heart of wisdom*" (v. 12), he flushes out what it means to live in the presence of God, day by day—to make God his dwelling place. In the context of a life of hardship, the psalmist finds a home, nevertheless, in the confines of God's love (v. 14). It is more than enough to satisfy his longing heart. Maybe the promised land was more about the promise than the land, in the end—a promise God fulfills with himself, anywhere. In the spacious parameters God sets for us, gladness comes in equal measure to the hardship that came before (v. 15). Our joy will exceed our days of mourning and grief (1 Peter 1:6–9). The work of our hands will not be toil, but delight, an extension of God's blessing on us and for others. His purposes will be fulfilled in us and will have a lasting (eternal) impact (v. 17). Moses has reoriented his understanding of life in God to see his reality from a new perspective. Deuteronomy 34:7 says that Moses died with his eyes *"undimmed and his vigor unabated."* At the end of his life, he clearly saw his life wrapped up in God's—where he dwelt in peace and satisfaction, despite unachieved goals, disappointment, and failures. The man who begged God for his presence received God's promise and dwelt in his presence to his last days (Exodus 33:14–15). The friendship of God was his reward (Exodus 33:11).

This is our reality, too, through the Lord Jesus Christ. Our circumstances do not have to define our lives. We can choose to understand our lives with godly wisdom. We can live with joy, gladness, and purpose, no matter what trial we face. Jesus, who lives in the hearts of those who love and receive him, is God's dwelling place (John 1:14). He is our home (John 14:23). He has guaranteed that our joy will exceed our days of affliction (John 16:20, 22). Let us pray for eyes undimmed, for eyes enlightened, that we may see his reality—his power and creativity and goodness—changing our mindset, if not our immediate scenery. We have received our reward. He is worth more than all the treasures this world has to offer (Hebrews 11:26). He is more than enough. He is.

REFLECTION:

What promise are you waiting for God to fulfill? What if it does not turn out the way you thought? What will you believe about God's promise?

DAY 30

MY PORTION FOREVER

Read Psalm 73.
Psalm 73 traces the critical path every heart must follow from bitterness to praise. Asaph, the author, weighs the evidence of his material circumstances against evidence for God and struggles to find his place. As if searching for God in the ruins of his life, the psalmist struggles with envy, bitterness, and despair. It is a dangerous and inevitable slide downwards from one to another. But as the opening line affirms, God is good to the pure in heart, who will always find God (Matthew 5:8) and be found by him. This psalm is a reorientation, of sorts. Through the grace of God, the psalmist finds the sanctuary of God and a new understanding of his reality.

Asaph poses an age-old question. Why do the wicked prosper? Where is God while they thrive, enjoying the pleasures of this material life? He is looking for evidence of a righteous and just God. He presents this as a problem, spending eight verses complaining about it. But the real problem for the psalmist is the condition of his heart. He is envious of those whose behavior is an affront to God (v. 3). It is easy for a lax heart to gaze upon the comfortable ease, elegance, and wealth of others and think they have it all. Power, popularity, and pleasures. Though the "wicked" are arrogant (v. 3), violent (v. 6), gluttons (v. 7), and scoffers of God (v. 8, 11) who oppress the weak (v. 8), the righteous writer still envies their status in society. This is the problem.

As one sin begets another, his envy quickly dissolves into self-pity—a temporarily satisfying temptation that feeds our petulant appetite (v. 13). By verse 14, the psalmist has completely forgotten his history with God—the faithful provision, steadfast love, and saving acts of grace: *"For all the day long I have been stricken and rebuked every morning."* Not only is his statement illogical and generally untrue, but he has also rushed to judgment, conceded the outcome before it has had time to play out according to God's design. He puts everything on the line. *"All in vain have I kept my heart clean"* (v. 13). His entire experience of faith, his whole existence as a child of God, seems like a waste compared to the fatted and perverse lives of those who persist in disregarding God. No wonder his soul is embittered (v. 21), and he teeters on despair (v. 16). Blaming God is a fruitless endeavor. Once God is no longer trusted, it is a quick fall to the bottom. Yes, the wicked prosper in the material world, for a time. Something is out of order in God's perfectly designed universe. That problem is sin. We live with the repercussions of it, but it does not have to shape our reality. Our reality with God is hope, not despair, satisfaction, not want.

It seems as if the psalmist haphazardly stumbles into the sanctuary of God and is revived to his senses. But as we will see, it is more likely the gracious act of God bringing him home. Verse 17 is the critical turning point upon which the psalmist regains his perspective of his life in God. Just as God's dwelling place is not a place but a person, so it is with his sanctuary.[24] It is the place where our heart is drawn to his. In verse 24, we find the Lord guides the sinner with his own hand and receives (envelops) him into his glory. There we are safe, at rest, and drawn to worship. God's gracious movement towards us always brings us back to himself (v. 24).

As Christians, we can enter that sanctuary anytime through faith in our Lord Jesus. Indeed, the sanctuary is within us. Hebrews 10:19–22 says that we may draw near to God through Christ, who opened the way for us. Ephesians 2:22 attests that the temple, the holy sanctuary of God, is within us, and Christ is the cornerstone. We can enter the holy sanctum with God anytime we find ourselves careening down a dangerous path of despair and hopelessness. Our slightest act of worship—a prayer, a song, a bended knee, an act of service opens the door.

At the onset of the psalm, the psalmist struggled to find the meaning of the world, apart from God (v. 16). Now, he easily discerns it in God's presence (v. 17). The psalmist has arrived at his new understanding where he can see his circumstance more clearly. He is lifted and sustained by God's hand (v. 23). He is not only guided with God's wise counsel but also drawn into the very bosom of God—received like a bride into the groom's arms (v. 24). The psalmist sees clearly that there is nothing the world offers that can satisfy his heart like God (v. 25). He has found that the joy of God's presence expands exponentially—it is ever increasing. The pleasures of the world, however, are ever diminishing. God is our portion (v. 26). Nothing in this created world can fill our hearts like the One who created them.

While we survey the evidence of the world around us, we remember the evidence of God—the resurrected life of Christ. God always raises up and brings glory to those who desire to find a refuge from the scornful world, to slip out of this upside-down, out-of-sync world to find his sanctuary. There we know the love of Christ that surpasses knowledge, and we are filled with all the fullness of God (Ephesians 3:19). Nothing can rival this peace. It is our evidence. It is our reality, and it is ours in the breath of a prayer.

REFLECTION:

Read Galatians 1:13–17. In this passage, Paul spends time comparing his choice to follow Christ with his former life. He wrote that he had been "*set apart before I was born*" and that the one "*who called me by his grace was pleased to reveal his Son to me.*" How are these words an encouragement to you when you consider the cost to follow Christ?

DAY 31

JOY COMES

Read Psalm 30.
In this Thanksgiving Psalm, we sense we are in an upward movement, still transitioning out of the Laments. Though there are still many images of death, they are viewed in retrospect. God has changed the circumstance. God has heard the cry. David extols God's nature to save and sketches a framework for the resurrected life that would come through Jesus.

Psalm 30 is still shrouded in the dark metaphors of the grave, with references to Sheol, the pit, mourning, and sackcloth. And yet, it is also an exuberant declaration of praise because God has radically changed the focus. In the first three verses, David describes the action of God. *"You have drawn me up"* (v. 1), *"you have healed me"* (v. 2), and *"you have brought up my soul"* (v. 3). We are drawn into the upward and positive movement of David's praise. What was once death is now restored life.

This pattern of life and death exhibits itself everywhere in the universe. The dark of night ends with the light of day. The dead flower buried in the winter ground emerges to new life in the spring. What begins in the darkness of a womb ends in new light of life in a mother's arms. Endings are the point of new beginnings. God has planted his essential character trait—bringing life out of death—into the universe. There is an order in his sovereignty; joy comes after sorrow.

David takes this understanding of renewal to a deeper level. It is much more personal than just a sunrise, a springtime flower, or a butterfly. What is seen in the universe is experienced in our individual lives. David demonstrates this with a personal account: first, life (v. 6–7a), then a death of sorts, (v. 7b–10), then new life (v. 11–12). The cycle is completely dependent upon God. Life is only good by God's favor (v. 7a). When God hides his face, joy departs (v. 7b). The lack of God's presence is the equivalent of death, the pit, and dust (v. 9). Only God can change this course, because only God can restore his favor and his presence. Hence, David cries for mercy in verse 10. Just as predictable as the sun rising, God hears David's cry (v. 2) and turns his weeping into joy (v. 5). For David, God orchestrates the movement of sorrow to joy.

However merciful this action may have been to David personally, as Christians we understand this pattern is broader and more gracious than we can imagine. This movement from sorrow to joy was meant for all mankind. The God who delighted to fill the earth with beauty, creativity, goodness, and love, desires that we would not languish in the pain and sorrow of life that comes through sin and death. He made a way out of suffering into a new experience of joy. It is not a false, fabricated feeling that disguises or masks pain. It is a genuine change—even power—that fills our spirit based on the work of Jesus Christ (Romans 15:13).

The movement from suffering to joy is the pattern that happened once in the life, death, and resurrection of Jesus, and now daily, momentarily, for all who believe in him. It is a way of life. Jesus entered life, suffered, and died on the cross for our sakes, and rose from the dead. His new life that lives in us is our joy. When the disciples who witnessed the tortuous, violent death of Jesus saw him alive, they understood that all of God's promises—salvation, resurrection, new life—were true (Matthew 28:8; Luke 24:41, 52). When we understand that he has conquered sin and death and lives in us, we understand that our outcome has changed. Sin does not rule us. Suffering and pain are not our destiny. Death is not the end of the story. Joy comes on the other side of it. After mourning, there will be dancing, (v. 11) after weeping, rejoicing (v. 5). This is the pattern of life God wants for us. Joy is his expectation for us.

It is still true that while we are in this world, we will experience pain and suffering. However, we have the sure promise that God, through Jesus, is changing that. Joy comes both now, through his Spirit, and in the days to come when his promise is ultimately fulfilled.

Jesus said to his disciples:

> *"Truly, truly, I say to you, you will weep and lament, but the world will rejoice. You will be sorrowful, but your sorrow will turn into joy. When a woman is giving birth, she has sorrow because her hour has come, but when she has delivered the baby, she no longer remembers the anguish, for joy that a human being has been born into the world. So also you have sorrow now, but I will see you again, and your hearts will rejoice, and no one will take your joy from you."*
>
> JOHN 16:20–22

Joy, ushered in by the Spirit, changes our experience of our suffering and pain (John 15:11; 1 Thessalonians 1:6). This assures us that it is from God. Our joy is not based on circumstances but on the living presence of Jesus in us. In it, we experience the comfort and strength of his fellowship in a fuller measure (1 Peter 4:12–13; Philippians 3:10). In Jesus, God's face is never hidden from us, nor is his favor ever removed from us. We always have his joy because he is always in us. Whatever suffering we are called to endure for a short time is the sure evidence that God's joy is coming (2 Corinthians 4:17). In faith, we rejoice in Jesus—wipe off the ashes, throw off the sackcloth—and let his gladness and joy fill us. It will be our greatest act of faith demonstrated to the world. Joy comes.

REFLECTION:

Do you have a personal history in which God has moved you from grief to joy? If so, use this space to remember how God has saved you, and then give thanks to him.

Do you have a painful story in which you need God to act? Present it in prayer to God now and ask Jesus for his joy to fill you even in the midst of it.

DAY 32

GOD'S LOVE FOR THE UNGREAT

Read Psalm 138.
David often expresses such lofty and transcendent ideas about God that we have to stretch our minds to understand his meaning. In Psalm 138, however, David voices a genuine sweetness and humility that makes it especially accessible to the reader. It is a very personal psalm—not from a king or victorious warrior, nor from a world leader or dignitary—but from the heart of a person who has felt weak, belittled, and lowly in spirit. Psalm 138 is a song for the "ungreat."[25] It is for us.

In this psalm, David emphasizes God's particular interest and care for himself. Seven times David uses the words "me" or "my." In verse 3, he declares, *"you answered me."* In verse 7, he asserts, *"your right hand delivers me."* In verse 8, he trusts, *"the Lord will fulfill his purpose for me."* Despite the holy and exalted nature of God (v.2), his love and faithfulness impacts David personally, as it does for all of us. Psalm 138 reminds us that God intended his transcendent goodness, including his salvation, to be accessible to every person, of high and low estate. We can easily slip into David's prayers and hear the comforting words over our own lives.

David expounds on another essential element of God's nature in verse 6: *"For though the LORD is high, he regards the lowly."* Just as he did in Psalm 8, considering the greatness of the Lord causes David to confront his own relative lowliness. For David, "God's greatness is seen in his regard for the ungreat."[26] Psalm 113 picks up on this same theme. *"He raises the poor from the dust and lifts the needy from the ash heap"* (Psalm 113:7). Part of God's character is that, though he is exalted above the heavens, he has a disproportionate concern for the small, the insignificant and weak. The stories of Jesus's life demonstrate this facet emphatically—how much more so, his death on the cross for us who are so inherently fragile and spiritually frail. We do not have to be the material poor to have been weak in crisis, belittled by others, taken advantage of, or poor in spirit. We have all been "ungreat" more times that we care to remember. But God increases the *"strength of our soul"* despite what little we have to warrant his attention. His favor for us is an aspect of his steadfast love and faithfulness (v. 2).

David establishes an effective model to give thanks to God by building a history of God's faithfulness. He specifically recounts what God has done for him, as if to see it with his own eyes. God answered his cry (v. 3), increased his strength (v. 3), preserves his life (v. 7), protects him from the enemy, delivers him (v. 7), and fulfills him (v. 8). It is an impressive and convincing list. We, too, can create a portfolio of the ways God has acted in our lives. The Bible is full of such accounts. In fact, God's people were commanded to remember the faithfulness of God over generations, from the dynamic movements of the Old Testament—the Passover, the Exodus, and the extraordinary events in the lives of the Prophets—to the miraculous signs and wonders of Jesus in the New Testament—culminating in his death, resurrection, and ascension (1 Chronicles 16:12; 2 Timothy 2:8). Peter, Stephen, and Paul insisted that their listeners remember what they saw, what they knew to be true. When God's actions throughout history align with the concrete evidence of our lives, his faithfulness to us becomes evident. We can believe he will act accordingly in the future. Our faith grows on the evidence of God's personal encounter in our own lives.

God is not an esoteric idea that floats somewhere above the galaxies. God is engaged in a personal interaction with us that generates first-hand information. David can say that God is good, because God has been good to him. He can say that God is caring and compassionate, because God has cared for him in his time of need. It is not speculation. As we consider God's real presence and action in our lives, it draws our heart to worship, as David does in the opening line: "*I give thanks, O LORD, with my whole heart; before the gods I sing your praise.*" God's behavior to us impacts our behavior to him. "*We love because he first loved us*" (1 John 4:19). As we remember Jesus's great love and powerful works for us—the inherently ungreat—let us join our voices with the psalmist:

> "*I will sing to the LORD, for he has been good to me.*"
>
> **PSALM 13:6, NIV**

REFLECTION:

Use the space below to make a list of all the ways God has been good to you. (You may need more pages... and it could take a lifetime.)

DAY 33

RADIANT FACES

Read Psalm 34.
Psalm 34 correlates to a time of fear, anxiety, and desperation in David's life. The superscription tells us it refers to the painful ordeal when David fled from King Saul who sought to kill him. David thought he could hide in enemy territory, but he was recognized due to his fame among the Philistines as a warring leader. Fearing that the king of Gath would seek to put him to death, David feigned insanity to persuade the king for his release. In perhaps one of his lowest and most undignified moments, David assumed the role of a madman. *"David... was much afraid of Achish the king of Gath. So he changed his behavior before them and pretended to be insane in their hands and made marks on the doors of the gate and let his spittle run down his beard"* (1 Samuel 21:12–13). A most inglorious memory for him, no doubt. Fear has a way of defacing us, bringing us to shameful actions. But God, in his mercy, delivers us not only from our enemy, but from the fear that distorts his glorious image in us. For this, David makes his song of thanksgiving.

In our previous psalms, we learned that God's salvation is uniquely tailored to our personal need. His rescue brings us joy even in the most difficult circumstances. Psalm 34 picks up this same theme, highlighting another facet. God's salvation produces change, not just in the circumstance but also in the person. In Psalm 34, David describes his transformation as a result of God's saving action. In comparison to the man of 1 Samuel 21, who play-acted a starving, drooling lunatic, assailed by fear, read his account of himself in God's hands:

> *"I sought the LORD, and he answered me and delivered me from all my fears.*
> *Those who look to him are radiant,*
> *and their faces shall never be ashamed.*
> *This poor man cried, and the LORD heard him*
> *and saved him out of all his troubles.*
> *The angel of the LORD encamps around those who fear him,*
> *and delivers them.*
> *Oh, taste and see that the LORD is good!*
> *Blessed is the man who takes refuge in him!*
> *Oh, fear the LORD, you his saints,*
> *for those who fear him have no lack!*

> *The young lions suffer want and hunger;*
> *but those who seek the LORD lack no good thing."*

PSALM 34:4–10

God's salvation has altered David's countenance and behavior completely. God has delivered David from all his fears (v. 4). His fear has been shifted from the enemy and been converted to awe, reverence, and trust in God. As a result, he is provided proper sustenance (v. 9–10). He trusts the Lord's angel to protect him, though the enemy is all around (v. 7). His perspective is positive and hopeful (v. 8). And most noticeably, his face is radiant and unashamed (v. 5). God's uplifting salvation brings dignity and honor and glory, especially to those who have suffered under the governance of their own fearful decisions.

God's salvation, which comes fully in Jesus Christ, changes us completely. The alteration is not a superficial makeover that only lingers for a time. It is not a momentary glow that lights up our face after a spiritual high, fading as we come down the mountain (2 Corinthians 3:13). It does not depend on our own efforts to clean up our lives. It is a transformation on the inside, in our spirit. Paul says, "*if anyone is in Christ, he is a new creation. The old has passed away; behold, the new has come*" (2 Corinthians 5:17). A new Spirit, that of the Lord Jesus Christ, has replaced our old one, and it will be evident in our actions, as well as our faces. We see this development in David, as he instructs others to fear of the Lord, guard their words, refrain from evil, do good, and seek peace (v. 11–14). We must believe that his own actions are true to his words, otherwise he would be a poor instructor. The most convincing saints are those who have come through a great ordeal, not with a bitter spirit, but with the light of God. Their actions confirm their transformation has happened from the inside out.

Our greatest witness to the world concerning the power of Christ will be the evidence of our lives. How we respond to trials and hardships, how we live out our days, the words we speak, and the love we exhibit will be the proof that Jesus lives. The light others see in our faces is the glory of Christ living in us (2 Corinthians 3:17–18). And that light is especially evident against the darkness (2 Corinthians 4:6). We do not need to fear the darkness, or the ordeal, the humiliating trial, or the shameful mistakes. God uses each of these to precipitate his beautiful new creation in us. In fact, God's glory is more evident in the face of them.

> "*But we have this treasure in jars of clay, to show that the surpassing power belongs to God and not to us. We are afflicted in every way, but not crushed; perplexed, but not*

driven to despair; persecuted, but not forsaken; struck down, but not destroyed."

2 CORINTHIANS 4:7-9

God's power displayed in our weakness will be our most obvious witness to the world. So let us boast in the Lord (v. 2), for *"those who look to him are radiant, and their faces shall never be ashamed"* (v. 5).

"The Son is the radiance of God's glory and the exact representation of his being, sustaining all things by his powerful word."

HEBREWS 1:3

REFLECTION:

Can you think of someone who has come through a difficult ordeal with a stronger witness for God? How does that person exhibit God's glory?

DAY 34

THE LORD REIGNS

Read Psalm 96.
I love to hear someone humming a tune to themselves. It makes me smile to see someone singing alone in their car. Maybe because I so often do those things. I often wonder what they sing about and why. I have determined from my own experience that a spontaneous song comes from an inner well of emotion that erupts when feelings are strong. It unites the body and spirit into one harmony. Very often, our singing draws others into the celebration, particularly if our song is joyous, victorious, and hopeful. It is hard not to join in. Psalm 96 invites us into such a song—a praise that comes after the trial, a joy that comes after the weeping. The new song celebrates the new life (as in Psalm 34) that has been born from God's salvation—not just in us, but throughout creation. It feels good to unite our whole being to this song that rings throughout the universe.

Psalm 96 is a very public expression. This is not a song to hum in the shower, sing alone in the car, or muffle quietly under our breath. This song broadcasts God's glory from the rooftops and draws every living being into it. Psalm 96 is a song for *"all the earth,"* as the psalmist says in the opening verse. It is for all nations (v. 3), *"all the peoples"* (v. 3), *"families"* (v. 7), the *"heavens"* (v. 11), and all creation (v. 11–12). The proclamation is not exclusive—it is meant for every ear to hear, and every voice to sing.

What are we to sing? Verse 2 tells us that we can begin by blessing the Lord's name and telling of his salvation day to day. Sing for who God is and what he does, day in and day out in our ordinary lives. God's nature (*"his name,"* v. 8) is manifested in his action (*"his marvelous works,"* v. 3) in the world. Here, in Psalm 96, the psalmist wants us to recognize the greatest, most glorious work of God is his salvation (v. 2). His salvation is recreating the world. We are adept at looking at his natural creation and seeing his *"splendor and majesty,"* his *"strength and beauty"* (v. 6). As the Creation Psalms affirm, God's glory is obvious and ostentatious in the sky, the mountains, the forests, the seas, the flora, the fauna, and everything he created. But even more remarkable is his salvation of people and families and nations. He is renewing and remaking our nature (each of us individually, one at a time) to reflect his glory, day in and day out—infusing his majesty and splendor into our lives. Something new is happening in the world and we are being swept up into it by his grace. We sing because that new way is welling up inside of us and we find our whole being is in harmony with it.

As we find ourselves caught up in the fanfare, we hear the refrain "*The LORD reigns!*" (v. 10). The song we are singing is a coronation song, and we are part of the great procession.[27] "*He comes*," sings the psalmist in verse 13. Psalm 96 announces the coming of the king who saves. There is to be a new reign and a new world order. Under his righteous and just rule, the Lord, who is king and also judge, will establish a government of equity (v. 10) and peace (Isaiah 9:7). No more will the old, sinful, and rebellious forces have power. People are freed from the oppressive regime that takes captives into its dark and twisted schemes. This is the basis for our triumphant march. It is happening now, but there is more to come.

When Jesus came to the world, he ushered in the kingdom of God. Yet, he instructed us to wait for his kingdom to come in its entirety (Matthew 24; Acts 1:7-8). How will we know when this new world order will take place? That is a question the disciples of Jesus fervently pressed upon their rabbi. John the Baptist sent a message to Jesus, inquiring, "*Are you the one who is to come?*" Jesus replied, *"Go and tell John what you have seen and heard: the blind receive their sight, the lame walk, lepers are cleansed, and the deaf hear, the dead are raised up, the poor have good news preached to them"* (Luke 7:19, 22). How will we know when the king has come and assumed his authority and power? We will know by what we see and hear. We will know by the work of his hands, in our daily lives. We will know by the evidence of salvation in our own hearts and in others. We will know by the evidence of the song rising up in us. Our heart will throb to cry out, "*He reigns!*"

The world still waits for the final advent of the king. We do not yet see all nations ascribing glory to God. His righteous judgment of all peoples has not been fully enacted. We long for natural creation to be freed from its perverse bondage (Romans 8:20–21). Our hearts are still wayward and slow to obey. So, we wait. But we wait with hope (Romans 8:25), for Jesus has given us his Spirit as a deposit, guaranteeing there is more to come (Ephesians 1:14). His Spirit is the evidence that the kingdom is alive and well in us (Luke 17:21). It is the means by which we believe, even know, that Christ reigns. Under Jesus's sovereign rule, we can experience his righteousness, justice, and peace even now. For this we must sing. For the kingdom within us, let us join with every living creature in heaven and on earth and under the earth and in the sea, and all that is in them (Rev. 5:13). Let us sing to Jesus. Let us sing of the king who reigns in us!

REFLECTION:

When have you felt <u>compelled</u> to sing? What was your state of mind? What happened to bring you to such a desire to sing? How is singing your thoughts different than saying them?

DAY 35

HOLY IS HE

Read Psalm 99.
Psalm 99 begins with the same refrain as Psalm 96, "*The LORD reigns*." This Enthronement Psalm continues to develop the idea of a righteous and just king who brings a new rule upon the earth. The psalmist is weaving together a portrait of God who is the supreme ruler over the earth and its peoples. For the psalmist, the king who comes is not only righteous and just (v. 4), but he is holy (v. 3, 5, 9). God alone meets these standards. There is no other king who is fully righteous, just, and holy—nor has there ever been. Unlike Psalm 96, this song is not sung from the rooftops. It is sung at the foot of the altar. This song is our call to worship.

We remember from Psalm 29 that the entrance of a holy God into our finite and fragile existence causes a disruption. He comes with force. In the first verse, we see the "*peoples tremble*." The earth quakes. When the holy king arrives on the scene, he shakes loose the power structures that hold the earth and its peoples in its grip.[28] As disconcerting, even frightening as this is, his sheer holiness—his purity cloaked in power—rises above them, generating awe that drives them to praise (v. 2–3). In the presence of this holy king, all idolatrous foundations crumble. And yet, those gripped by his love find themselves not only safe in his presence but also made pure in themselves. This is the ground upon which he builds his new kingdom.

God, the holy king, comes to build his kingdom on earth. What will be the defining characteristics of such a kingdom? It will be established with equity, justice, and righteousness (v. 4–5). The prophet Isaiah described such a ruler and his kingdom:

> "*And the Spirit of the LORD shall rest upon him,*
> *the Spirit of wisdom and understanding,*
> *the Spirit of counsel and might,*
> *the Spirit of knowledge and the fear of the LORD.*
> *And his delight shall be in the fear of the LORD.*
> *He shall not judge by what his eyes see,*
> *or decide disputes by what his ears hear,*
> *but with righteousness he shall judge the poor,*
> *and decide with equity for the meek of the earth;*
> *and he shall strike the earth with the rod of his mouth,*

> *and with the breath of his lips he shall kill the wicked.*
> *Righteousness shall be the belt of his waist,*
> *and faithfulness the belt of his loins.*
> *The wolf shall dwell with the lamb,*
> *and the leopard shall lie down with the young goat,*
> *and the calf and the lion and the fattened calf together;*
> *and a little child shall lead them."*
>
> ISAIAH 11:2–6

We join our voice with the psalmist and with the Lord Jesus who embodied Isaiah's vision, saying, "*thy kingdom come, thy will be done in earth, as it is in heaven*" (Matthew 6:10, KJV). But we do not say this lightly, for this prayer is revolutionary. It will turn our lives upside down, and all false bottoms will drop.

The psalmist calls us to worship such a king who can bring universal peace. "*Exalt the LORD our God; worship at his footstool! Holy is he!*" (v. 5) He calls his people to be holy, so he calls us to himself. The psalmist calls us to worship at his footstool (v. 5), to worship at his holy mountain (v. 9). The images of an angelic host (v. 1), the pillar of cloud (v. 7), the tri-fold proclamation of holiness (v. 3, 5, 9) and the trembling foundations (v. 1) remind us somehow of Isaiah's experience in the temple (Isaiah 6:1–7). The Lord is in his temple. What will our song be?

The entrance of the holy king shatters our self-anointed realms. When the Lord decides to make himself known, he is obvious and unavoidable. He comes with power to shake the small kingdoms we have constructed for ourselves—our little dominions, our societal fiefdoms where we exercise authority and influence. He demolishes the temples we have built to wealth and smashes our idols of pleasure, leisure, and license to which we pay homage. He tears down our altars of self-pride and vanity. He has no regard for these trivial monarchies, the weak and unstable imitations that hold us captive. His presence brings the painful but necessary destruction, for the two kingdoms cannot stand together. So we face a choice: Hang on to the collapsing rubble and sing "*Woe is me*," or fling ourselves into his arms and cry, "*Here I am*" (Isaiah 6:5–8).

As our kingdoms fall, God reaches out his hand and lifts us to himself. We stand or kneel, or prostrate ourselves before the Holy God, but we do not do so alone. The Lord Jesus is with us. He has washed us (1 Corinthians 6:11), clothed us (Galatians 3:27), and anointed our heads (1 John 2:20, 27). Only Jesus's purifying presence can make us holy and blameless before the Lord (Philippians 1:10–11). Here we are, Lord—ready for the unshakeable kingdom you want to build in us, your kingdom of righteousness and peace. This is our first act of worship—to present our bodies as living sacrifices, holy and acceptable to God (Romans 12:1). Let us sing! Holy is he!

REFLECTION:

What must be shaken in you for the Lord to establish his reign more fully in your life? (See also Hebrews 12:25–29.)

NOTES

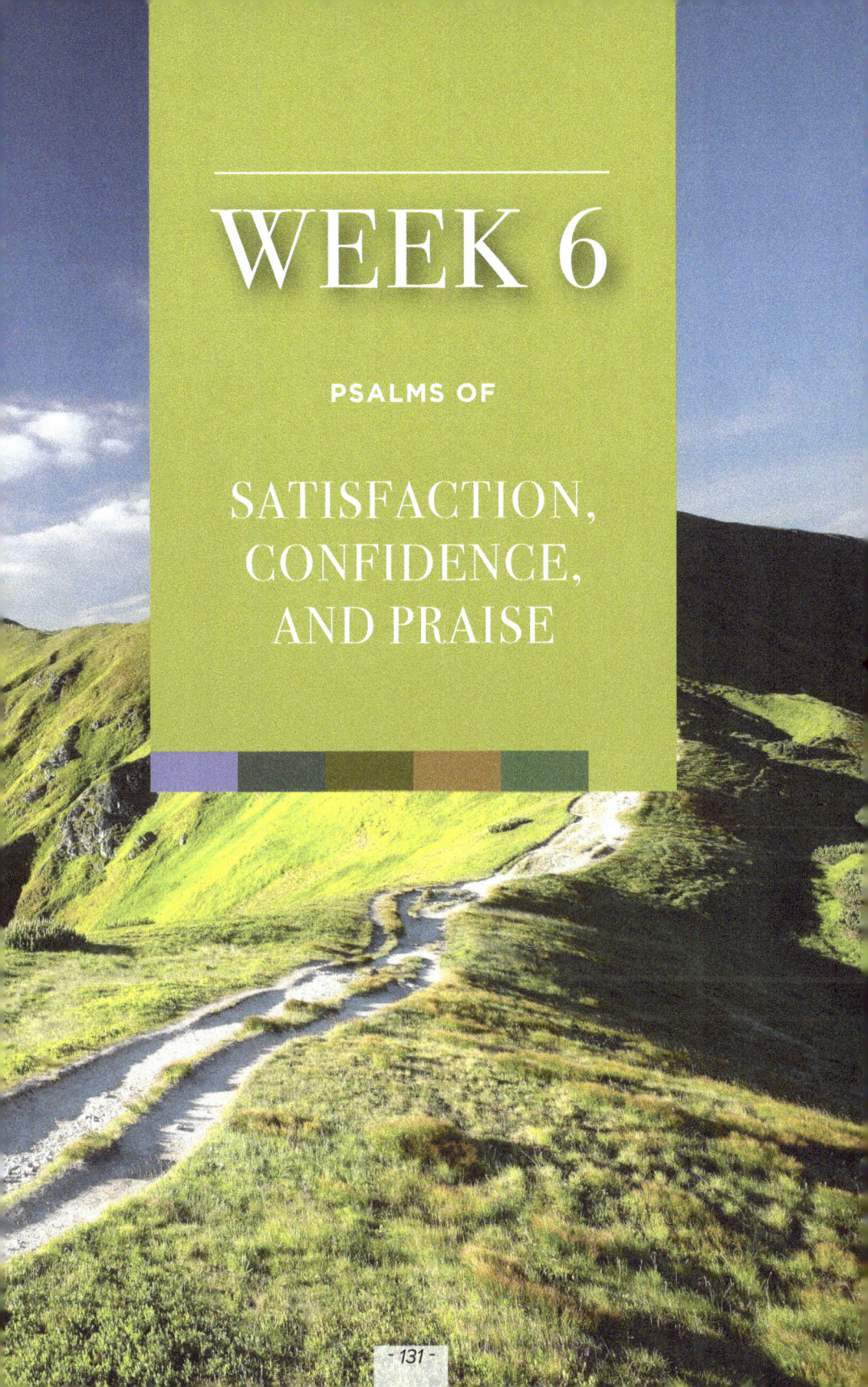

WEEK 6

PSALMS OF

SATISFACTION, CONFIDENCE, AND PRAISE

Introduction to the Psalms of Satisfaction, Confidence, and Praise

The psalms appointed for this lesson are some of the most recognized and most loved psalms in the collection. They present a deeply grounded and unwavering faith in God and his goodness. They convey a strong sense of confidence in God and his ability to resolve all circumstances. This confidence, in turn, provides a sense of satisfaction—even pleasure—found in God's presence. Psalms 23, 27, and 91 address the concept of fear, though no specific threat is mentioned. They build a broad and expansive structure that protects against every fear and enemy. The references to "*dwellings*," "*refuge*," "*sanctuary*," and the "*house of the LORD*" can all be seen as our relationship with Jesus Christ, a framework where provision, safety, and satisfaction are found.

The psalms at the end of the Psalter lead us to a state of praise. Despite the difficult and tortuous path we have climbed, we have arrived at a place where our soul discovers that our most appropriate stance before God is praise. These psalms seem to have come full circle from where we began, affirming the well-ordered life under God's rule and reign.[29] In this lesson, we will study four Psalms of Praise (Psalms 117, 103, 100, and 148). They are public songs, meant to summon others to worship. They are sung with an abandonment to God, for his character and action. They reflect a sense of wonder in God and the life he has designed for us in communion. They are exuberant, unrestrained, and flushed with joy. Not only do they model true worship, but they suggest a life in God that is to be characterized by joy. We are made for joy. As Christians, we experience that joy as a manifestation of the Spirit alive in us. Jesus said *"Remain in my love... I have told you this so my joy may be in you and that your joy may be complete"* (John 15:9–11, NIV). Only through Jesus can we truly find that joy and enter the worship for which we are made.

DAY 36

HIS FEATHERS AND FORTRESS

Read Psalm 91.
Psalm 91 captures us with the psalmist's sheer confidence and trust in God. One has the sense of having entered a war zone, with the threat of enemy attacks around every corner. In that sense, Psalm 91 accurately depicts a life where danger assails our security and peace—if not materially, then certainly spiritually. The psalmist does not portray a life without trouble, but a life of confidence in the face of it. The poetic language includes a broad array of threats: a snare, a deadly pestilence, a terror of the night, an arrow, a destruction, and a young lion (v. 3–13). Surely our fears have fallen into one of these categories, at one time or another. The reference to *"the young lion and the serpent"* makes it clear that these threats are the work of our spiritual enemy, Satan (v. 13; 1 Peter 5:8; Revelation 20:1). But the psalmist reveals his strength and protection to maneuver in such a hostile environment. He *"dwells in the shelter of the Most High"* (v. 1). His protection is his proximity.

The psalmist uses several images to depict the idea of shelter. *"Refuge,"* *"fortress,"* *"wings,"* *"shield,"* *"rampart"* (v. 4, NIV), and *"dwelling place"* all describe a state of protection that comes from proximity to God. In fact, God is the place of protection. Whoever dwells in him will be provided what is necessary for deliverance, rescue, honor, satisfaction, and salvation (v. 14–16). It is a promise that is secured by God's character. He is the Most High (*El Elyon*, the sovereign ruler of the universe, over all things) and the Almighty (*El Shaddai*, the all-sufficient God who pours forth and provides for all needs, who completely satisfies). This is who he is and what he does. The promise is ultimately delivered by his Son, Jesus Christ.

To illustrate the power of God's proximity, the psalmist uses two strikingly different images: a fortress (v. 2) and feathers (v. 4). First, the picture of the fortress fits with the psalm's war zone references: *"snare,"* *"shield,"* *"buckler"* (or *"rampart"*), *"arrow,"* and *"tent."* When a warrior is in battle, looking for protection, he might lean his back against a wall of a fortress to shield himself from a barrage of incoming fire—bullets, arrows, stones. There he can hide himself, shield himself, and catch his breath. His protection comes from his proximity to the wall, while moving away from the wall exposes him to the attack. He and the wall are one.

The second image is found in verse 4. *"He will cover you with his pinions (feathers, NIV) and under his wings you will find refuge."* The Lord protects like a mother bird who shelters her young under her wings. Nestled close to the bosom of God, safety and refuge are found. The root word of El Shaddai (the name for God translated "*Almighty*" in verse 1) is the Hebrew word "shad," meaning "breast." With that image comes the implication of power, provision, and satisfaction. Accounts are known of barnyard birds who, in the event of a fire, will shelter their young under their wings, even to the point of death, so that the fledglings will live. Jesus used this same image in Matthew 23:37 as he contemplated the coming fire of judgment. The fortress conveys strength and power. The wing depicts love and nurture. Together we have a beautiful picture of provision that comes by a deeply intimate posture in God's presence.

How do we abide in this strong and sheltered presence of God? Jesus taught his disciples this vital concept when he explained his relationship with the Father. They were one, Jesus said. When Philip asked Jesus to see the Father, Jesus's response was, "*Whoever has seen me has seen the Father*" (John 14:9). In his parting prayer with the disciples, Jesus asserts that he is one with the Father, and that his believers will be drawn into that same relationship. "*Just as you, Father, are in me, and I in you, that they also may be in us*" (John 17:20). Jesus told us how to dwell with the Father. "*Abide in me*" (John 15:4). Jesus is the dwelling place. We do not merely have proximity to the fortress, we are in the fortress, and he is in us. Because he has defeated all powers and dominions that rage against us, including sin and death, because he lives forever and reigns above all things, we are forever protected by him and his love for us.

> "*If God is for us, who can be against us?*
> *He who did not spare his own Son but gave him up for us all,*
> *how will he not also with him graciously give us all things?*
> *Who shall bring any charge against God's elect?*
> *Who shall separate us from the love of Christ?*
> *Shall tribulation, or distress, or persecution, or famine,*
> *or nakedness, or danger, or sword?*
> *No, in all these things we are more than conquerors*
> *through him who loved us. For I am sure that neither death*
> *nor life, nor angels nor rulers, nor things present nor things to*
> *come, nor powers, nor height nor depth, nor anything else in*
> *all creation, will be able to separate us from the love of God in*
> *Christ Jesus our Lord.*"
>
> ROMANS 8:31–33, 35, 37–39

Psalm 91 does not promise a life free from trouble. It suggests the opposite. But it does promise that God will be with us, and we will be safe in him, come what may. God's promise, accomplished in Jesus, is this: *"Because he holds fast to me in love, I will deliver him… I will satisfy him and show him my salvation"* (v. 14, 16). Jesus said, *"I have told you these things, so that in me you may have peace. In this world you will have trouble. But take heart! I have overcome the world"* (John 16:33, NIV). Therefore, we can go forward in confidence, and strength, holding fast to the Lord in love.

REFLECTION:

What fear has a grip on you, attacking your peace and well-being? How can you remain in Jesus? Where can you find his strength (fortress wall) and his comfort (protective wing)?

DAY 37

ONE THING

Read Psalm 27.
In this psalm of confidence and trust, David prays, "*Teach me your way, O LORD, and lead me on a level path because of my enemies*" (v. 11). We are the beneficiaries of such an instruction in Psalm 27. It ushers us into the refuge that awaits all who seek the Lord, even in the midst of adversaries (v. 2), while war rises up all around (v. 3). Though real danger encamps around him, David is confident (v. 3). The presence of the Lord is a place of immunity from fear, protection from enemies, and revelation of God's goodness and blessing.

In the threatening scene of Psalm 27, one would expect to find a fortress, as in Psalm 91. We are surprised, instead, by the images associated with worship. David describes the place where we dwell with the Lord as "*the house of the LORD*" and "*his temple*" (v. 4), "*his shelter*" and "*his tent*" (or "tabernacle," v. 5, NIV). In this place, he is hidden and concealed from his enemies. This image is like his thought in Psalm 23, where a banquet table is set in the presence of his enemies, perhaps even an altar, for it is also the place where he is anointed, and his cup is filled. In Psalm 91, David's protection came from his proximity to God. Here, his safety and security come as he enters the sanctuary in worship.

David was once called a man after God's own heart (Acts 13:22). Psalm 27 reveals David's heart of worship for the Lord. Of all the things a king could pray for under the onslaught of an enemy, David seeks only one thing: to be solely, intimately, unabashedly in the near presence of God. He prays with intensity, "*My heart says to you, 'Your face, LORD, do I seek'*" (v. 8). Is this not the kind of worshipper God has been seeking, one who is present to the Lord not just in body but also with entirety of spirit (John 4:23)? How often we enter the presence of the Lord distracted, captivated by the sights and sounds of worship but less with the object. Even in private prayer, our heads are full of peripheral noises and voices. It is hard to see his face if we are not looking for it. God has said, "*Seek my face*" (v. 8). When we do, the outside attacks dissipate instantly. How close can we approach? From the One who told Moses he could not see his face; we have been given access into the most holy sanctuary through his Son (Hebrews 10:19–21). What if we could approach so nearly that we could feel his warm, steady, rhythmic breath upon our forehead, assuring us of our privileged position (John 20:21–22; Psalm 131:2)? He wants us this close. Jesus gently chastised Martha for distraction, for the distance she kept even while she was serving the Lord. He told her, "*Only one thing is needed*" (Luke 10:42 NIV). He wants to be that one thing.

Enemies have a way of bringing us to worship. For this we can be thankful, in a strange kind of way. But their attacks do not come in neat, orderly times and places. We must learn to worship in battle, in combat, on the spot. In Jesus, we can do that. He was the temple, the dwelling place of the Lord on earth (John 2:19–22; John 1:14). When he ascended into heaven and sent the Holy Spirit, he came to live in us, making our bodies the temple where God's Spirit dwells (Ephesians 2:21–22; 1 Corinthians 6:19).

We have access to the upfront and personal presence of God instantly, everywhere. Hidden in his shelter, covered by his tent, we flourish in his presence (v. 13). We gaze on his beauty while arrows assail. We make sacrifices most dear with song. And no one suspects the joy that rises and expands in our hiding place (Psalm 32:7). In the midst of our danger, God has set our feet upon the rock and set our hearts free (v. 5; 1 Corinthians 10:4). He lifts our heads in the presence of our enemies and anoints them with his healing balm (v. 6; Psalm 23:5). Our enemies pressure us to bow before them, but our strength comes in bowing to the Lord. In that act, we are lifted up with honor and dignity (v. 6). We can know this kind of worship anywhere, for he goes with us. We are never separated from his intimate presence.

Let us join our heart and voice with the psalmist in Psalm 73:25: *"Whom have I in heaven but you? And there is nothing on earth that I desire besides you."* Lord Jesus, you are our one thing! Come be our one thing!

REFLECTION:

Sometimes we do not recognize that Jesus is all that we need until he is all that we have. Can you recall a time when this was true for you? How would you describe your relationship with God during that time?

Is there anything you are holding onto that takes Jesus's place? Consider saying a prayer and relinquishing that item or person to his purpose. Ask him to be your one thing.

DAY 38

HE LEADS ME

Read Psalm 23.
The well-known and well-loved Twenty-third Psalm settles any agitated heart with its sense of peace and contentment. These six short verses are very different from Psalms 91 and 27, with their depictions of war. Psalm 23 paints a bucolic scene with green pastures, still waters, and gentle pathways. The psalmist is so secure, he can safely lie down by the water without fear of attack. The reason for his confidence is the presence of the Lord. In Psalm 23, David offers another avenue for dwelling with the Lord. To experience the satisfying nearness of the Lord, we must surrender ourselves to his direction and will.

Psalm 23 presents a picture of a completely yielded spirit before the Lord. With each verse, we discover that David has put himself wholly in God's hands and power. In this personal prayer, we realize the primary subject is God, not the psalmist. It begins with "*The LORD*" and ends in "*house of the LORD.*" Every motion in the psalm is governed by the Lord.

He makes me...
He leads me...
He restores my soul...
He guides me...
You are with me...
You prepare a table before me...
You anoint my head...
Your goodness follows me...

God leads David to rest, refreshment, and righteousness (v. 2–3). God guides David through the dark places (v. 4) and provides for his every need, exceedingly (v. 5). God lifts him up, honors him, anoints him, and satisfies him completely (v. 6). God directs and David receives. It appears that David is simply along for the ride, and it is a good ride. David is completely yielded to the action of the Shepherd.

David's spiritual understanding has grown and matured from what he expressed in his Psalms of Lament. Psalm 23 shows a genuine willingness to be led. Though trouble and enemies lurk nearby, there is no complaint, no distress, no fear, and no lament (v. 4).

David does not complain that the way is too hard, or that he is too weak. He does not offer God alternatives, as if he had something else in mind. He does not question God's motives or the possible outcomes. What if he is hurt, suffers, or dies? These possibilities do not seem to be a consideration. David's well-being is wholly wrapped up in God's will for him. Perhaps it is the pattern of seeking the beauty of God's face alone (Psalm 27:4) that has dispersed all detracting thoughts (1 John 4:18).

We remember David's prayer from Psalm 27. "*Teach me your way, O LORD, and lead me on a level path*" (Psalm 27:11). When we submit ourselves to be taught, to be led, we find that God leads us straight to himself. For where has the path led David in this psalm? Straight to the table, the altar in the house of the Lord (v. 5–6). When we learn from God's Word and surrender to his path, suddenly we find the one thing that has been missing—proximity. Our submission is the entry point to the intimate worship that is so satisfying to our souls (v. 1, 6).

Psalm 23 presents a movement from the outside to the inside. The scene begins with a walk with the Shepherd, somewhere in the great wide pastures of life—through the threat of storms, famine, wild beasts, bandits, cold nights, and blistering days. And yet through all of this, the Shepherd guides, leads, protects, and comforts us along a path that leads to an interior scene—a place of refuge, fullness, extravagance, safety, and peace. God the shepherd leads us from the hinterlands into his inner sanctum—his heart. There is a way through the storms, through the treacherous conditions, even through the shadow of death (v. 4). Jesus, our Shepherd, is the way through to the Father's heart (John 10:11; 14:6).

David's trust in this psalm is remarkable. He does not doubt God in any measure. He does not question his own ability to get "through" because he is completely caught up in the movement of God. God is leading every step of the way. Jesus told the disciples that they would receive power when the Holy Spirit came upon them (Acts 1:8). We receive that same Spirit and power when we believe in Jesus. With that power, he equips us to follow where he leads, even and especially through difficult places. By the power of the Holy Spirit, we can go where we would never have ventured on our own (v. 4). We can rest when danger is on the prowl (v. 1). We can walk with confidence and honor in the midst of those who want to take us down (v. 5). To receive his power, we must be willing to receive. It is a yielding of our spirit to his. It is our invitation to let him lead.

Psalm 23 is a picture of complete fulfillment and satisfaction of life in God's presence. There is nothing we lack as we surrender ourselves to his abundant presence in our lives (v. 1). His desire is to fill us to overflowing with his goodness and love (v. 5–6). He wants to lead us through to this place that is his heart. Will we follow?

> *"My sheep hear my voice, and I know them, and they follow me."*
>
> **JOHN 10:27**

REFLECTION:

Which verse in this psalm speaks to a need in your life today? Consider memorizing that verse and make it a daily prayer request.

DAY 39

LOVE TOWARD US

Read Psalm 117.
Sometimes a writer is asked to explain the main message of her book in what is called an "elevator speech." The idea is to condense her ideas into several sentences that she could explain in the time it takes an elevator to go from the lobby to the upper floor. Others have said an author should be able to write the main idea on a cocktail napkin. As we come to the shortest psalm in the Psalter, we get the idea that the writer followed this advice. It is a summons to praise God. To list all the reasons to praise God would take us a lifetime and beyond, if it were possible. Maybe that is the point. In his wisdom, the psalmist has provided a summary that is direct, precise, yet all-encompassing. It serves as synopsis of the whole Psalter and the Bible as well.

The psalmist summons all nations and all people to praise the Lord. This directive carries us back to God's call to one man to draw one nation to God. When God called Abraham, part of the promise was that *"all peoples on earth"* would be blessed by God through him (Genesis 12:3, NIV). It was God's plan that all the nations of the earth would experience God's steadfast love and give praise in response to it. The Book of Revelation reveals a scene which is surely the culmination of God's beautiful plan.

> *"I looked, and behold, a great multitude that no one could number, from every nation, from all tribes and peoples and languages, standing before the throne and before the Lamb, clothed in white robes, with palm branches in their hands, and crying out with a loud voice, 'Salvation belongs to our God who sits on the throne, and to the Lamb!' And all the angels were standing around the throne and around the elders and the four living creatures, and they fell on their faces before the throne and worshiped God, saying, 'Amen! Blessing and glory and wisdom and thanksgiving and honor and power and might be to our God forever and ever! Amen.'"*
>
> REVELATION 7:9–12

The single-most praiseworthy characteristic of God is his steadfast love—his eternal, unwavering, persevering love for the people he created for himself. His love, which is sometimes translated *"merciful kindness"* (KJV) is so great that it extends to all people—good, bad, faithful, rebellious, blessed, hurt, healthy, sick, beautiful, unbeautiful, hopeful, despaired, capable, and unqualified. God's love calls people, who are not his people, to himself (Hosea 1:10; Romans 9:22–26). It always has.

God's love is not only expansive but also faithful. He takes into account the sinful weakness of people and provides a way for them to still be called holy, a *"people for his own possession"* (1 Peter 2:9–10). He refuses to leave us in our natural, degenerative state. In his unfailing perseverance, he never leaves us or forsakes us. Therefore, we are not left to ourselves but invited into the throng who will know and experience God's goodness and mercy forever. How can this be?

The single-most merciful act of kindness God ever exhibited was the life of Jesus Christ. God fulfilled his promise to bless all peoples of the earth through Jesus (Galatians 3:8, 14). The life of Jesus, offered to God on our behalf and for all people everywhere, brought the mercy of God to us. Through him, we can know God, experience his love, be cleansed from our sins, and draw near to him. In Jesus, we can live as God designed—now in part and forever fully. God acted out his faithful, extravagant love for us in the life of his Son Jesus. This is the reason for our unending praise.

In two short verses, the psalmist has summarized the entire Gospel of Jesus Christ and our purpose for life. Our job is to tell the world, tell the nations, tell our neighbor next door: God's love for you and me is great. This love is for everyone who desires it—near and far. No one deserves it, but he offers it to all. *"For God so loved the world, that he gave his only Son, that whoever believes in him should not perish but have eternal life"* (John 3:16). Praise the Lord!

REFLECTION:

Read Ephesians 1:3–10. For each verse, write out the action that God has taken for you, then write a prayer of praise for all God has done for you.

Example:

Verse 3:
He has blessed me with every spiritual blessing in the heavenly realms.

DAY 40

PRAISE CHANGES PERSPECTIVES

Read Psalm 103.
Many of us begin our day in prayer. With a hot cup of coffee, half-awake and unfocused, we try to gather our thoughts and direct them toward God. Many of us end our day in prayer. Reviewing the scenes of the day, our hearts are exhausted and worried. We try to redirect our wired brains from the events of the day to the One who stands over them. Sometimes we pray out of anger or fear, not sure where those thoughts are aimed. But we throw those prayers out there into God's universe, hoping that he understands them. In this seemingly haphazard and very organic process, a miracle is taking place. Our hearts are turned toward God and he enters that space and time to draw us to himself. Eugene Peterson wrote, "All prayer, pursued far enough, becomes praise."[30] That is the pattern that David displays to us in this exuberant psalm of praise, Psalm 103.

In this psalm of praise, David shows us the importance of being very intentional in our prayers. *"Bless the LORD, O my soul, and all that is within me, bless his holy name! Bless the LORD, O my soul, and forget not all his benefits"* (v. 1–2). David directs his attention to God's name (his character) and his benefits (his works). Praise is about who God is and what he does. We often use our feelings as a barometer for our ability to praise. We say we do not "feel" like it at the moment. We wonder if we can command the heart to feel things it does not. But praise has nothing to do with how we feel. It has only to do with acknowledging God. And we can do that anywhere. We are <u>called</u> to do that everywhere. *"Rejoice always, pray without ceasing, give thanks in all circumstances, for this is the will of God in Christ Jesus for you"* (1 Thessalonians 5:16–18). This shift in focus means we can truly praise God anywhere, under any circumstances. In sorrow, in sadness, in pain, and fear, we can proclaim who God is—and still find him good, powerful, loving, and victorious. He never changes. But we do. Our hearts change as we pray. God's character and power move us to praise him with all that is within us.

David begins this movement by contemplating God's works. He intentionally remembers what God has done (v. 2). It is an excellent and inspiring model. God's actions toward David form a litany that we can easily adopt. God forgives our sins, heals our diseases, and redeems our lives from *"the pit"* (v. 3–4). He crowns us with love and compassion, satisfies us with good things, and renews our vigor (v. 4–5). He works righteousness in us (v. 6). We can conclude that God's actions toward us are exceedingly extravagant. He knows that we are dust (v. 14), yet he condescends to forgive us and crown us with his love. *"He does not deal with us according to our sins"* (v. 10). His love is graciously unfair. His love is as *"high as the heavens"* (v. 11). His love is <u>on</u> us from *"everlasting to everlasting"* (v. 17). God's love is directed toward us and is always on us! Wow! His graciousness is overwhelming. David began his prayer by examining God's works, which led him to examine God's character. God is good to us. God is good.

As we pray alongside the psalmist, our hearts shift and we discover the extraordinary nature of prayer. God comes and fills the space and time with himself. Psalm 22:3 says that God is *"enthroned"* on the praises of his people. Some versions say he *"inhabits the praises"* of his people (KJV). Whatever version, the language expresses the infilling presence of God when we begin to praise him. As we acknowledge and agree with who God is, we align ourselves with his character. There is a unity of spirit, even communion with him. With the Spirit comes knowledge and truth of who God is, in ever-increasing degrees, and that revelation changes us. We emanate the Spirit. The Scriptures say we glow with it (2 Corinthians 3:18; 4:6). Our praise is a reflection, an expression, a release of his glory. If we want to have a fuller experience of God, praise is the entrance into the throne room of God.

That is exactly where David's prayers have landed. David sees that the king enthroned in his spirit is the same king who *"has established his throne in the heavens, and his kingdom rules over all"* (v. 19). He catches a glimpse of God's great, victorious reign, when he will come again in power, subjecting all kingdoms, powers, and authorities to Jesus. This happens to us in praise. We are given insight into God's eternal plan. On that day, all creation will sing God's praises, and his glory will be known throughout the earth. While we wait with eager expectation, we are the voice that declares the glory of God. We may be but one voice, but one voice lifted in praise awakens others. By our praise, others will catch the vision. Praise changes perspectives. Let us bless the Lord! With all that is within us, let us bless his holy name!

REFLECTION:

What perspective do you need to change? Consider praising God for everything you can think of regarding the issue. See how God changes your perspective and gives you a new vision.

DAY 41

O BE JOYFUL

Read Psalm 100.

"Make a joyful noise to the LORD!" In Psalm 100, the psalmist once again calls upon all the earth to worship the Lord. Exuberant celebration percolates in this psalm of praise, rising up and spilling over for all to partake. Joy and worship are the main posture and purpose for our life in God. The struggles to understand God and our place in creation have boiled down in God's faithful presence, leaving a rich and concentrated awareness that life with God is meant for joy. Our only response is worship, and the psalmist leads us in this simple and straightforward song. We praise and worship the Lord because he is God.

What kind of God is worthy of our complete praise, service, and worship? The psalmist tells us he is the LORD—Yahweh, the covenantal God in relationship with us, who always keeps his promises (v. 3). He is also the Creator God, the universal God over all creation. When we put these two concepts together, we are astounded by the prospect. The God over all creation, who spoke the world into being—who made the majestic mountains and the mighty thunderstorms that roll over them—this God wants to be in relationship with us, in a loving union of spirit and soul. He is the lover of his small but infinitely important creation.

The Creator God made us as he did everything else in the heavens and on the earth. *"It is he who made us"* (v. 3). He desired us before our birth, brought us into being, and drew us to himself, so that we may know his joy (Psalm 139:13–16). We can say like the psalmist, *"I praise you, for I am fearfully and wonderfully made. Wonderful are your works; my soul knows it very well"* (Psalm 139:14).

The covenantal God not only made us, but he also made us his own. *"The LORD is good; his steadfast love endures forever, and his faithfulness continues to all generations"* (v. 5). God's steadfast love and faithfulness keep us in relationship with him. Regardless of our waywardness, failings, and determination to go it alone, his love and faithful actions toward us remain (Psalm 139:7–12). His loving kindness enacted through Jesus makes us his own, *"his people, and the sheep of his pasture"* (v. 3; John 10:14).

Celebrating what God has done for us produces in us a sense of freedom, even unrestrained glee and pleasure. Praise is the outflow of that experience.[31] When we enjoy something, we naturally want to praise it. Joy brings us to that spontaneous eruption with which the psalmist begins this psalm. *"Make a joyful noise to the LORD, all the earth!"* (v. 1).

Do we have the freedom to truly experience the delight of God's presence? Many of us are reserved and feel awkward, uncoordinated, and silly experimenting with expressions of joy. Perhaps we remember our undistinguished, unselfconscious attempts of our childhood. Perhaps we knew something more then. Jesus said that the kingdom of heaven belongs to those with the abandon of children (Matthew 18:3). We must remember that joy produced by the Spirit is a gift to us (Galatians 5:22). We are called to celebrate God without restraint in our spirit and with our bodies. We are made for this pleasure!

What are we to do with our unrestrained joy? We are to direct it back to the God who gave it to us. *"Enter his gates with thanksgiving, and his courts with praise! Give thanks to him; bless his name!"* (v. 4). Worship becomes the consummation of joy.[32] This vision of worship and praise may be a foretaste of the fully liberated kingdom that Jesus will bring one day. At that time, joy will resound antiphonally throughout all creation—poured out by the Spirit, offered back to him in praise (Psalm 98:7–9). But we do not have to wait. The world knows nothing of the joy Jesus has for us. He has promised it to us and says that no one can take it from us (John 16:22). We can ask for his joy to be made complete in us (John 16:24). What are we waiting for? We have the Spirit now, who fills us with joy (Acts 13:52) and we have the freedom to live in it (2 Corinthians 3:17). Let us shout to the Lord with joy. Let us come into his presence with singing. For the Lord is good. His steadfast love endures forever. We are made for this.

REFLECTION:

When do you feel completely free to worship the Lord with your body and your spirit? Describe what those moments are like.

How can you pursue more joy in your life?

DAY 42

A HORN FOR HIS PEOPLE

Read Psalm 148.
As we come to the end of the Psalter, we are surrounded by choruses of voices, resounding throughout the heavens and the earth, as if reverberating off the clouds and the waters, and filling all space and time with praise for God. Our heads and hearts ring with their insistent summons to join the praise, for it is meant to be sung in unison. All creation is singing in a unity of spirit, creating a "oneness" that defines this psalm. The unity of all creation, free to sing and to worship God, envisions the full and final establishment of God's kingdom. It is an anthem for the new king who arrives in power.

The first verses ring from the highest heights (v. 1). Angels, angelic armies, and even the sun, moon, and stars join in. Even the mysterious reference to the "*highest heavens*" (v. 4) shows that nothing in the created order, above and over the earth, is excluded from the call to praise God. All have been created by God and commanded to praise (v. 5). Scriptures teach us that the angels are always singing (Isaiah 6:3–4; Luke 2:13–14; Revelation 4:8–11). Though we do not imagine the sun and the moon and the stars to sing, Charles Spurgeon poetically suggests how this could be possible. "Their light is praise in visible form. Light is song glittering before the eye instead of resounding in the ear."[33] These heavenly bodies initiate this psalm of praise for the rest of creation.

In the wake of the joyous heavenly refrain, the psalmist addresses the earthly realm. Like the heavens, all earthly creation is called to join the song. The sea and its creatures are joined with the elements of fire, wind, mist, hail, and snow. Nothing in all creation is excluded. Mountains and the trees on them, hills and the beasts roaming them, must take their part. Birds are added and then "*creeping things*" (v. 10), as if the comprehensive task of naming everything has finally brought this list to a general end. Then, with a drumroll, humankind is called into the great anthem. From the greatest to the least, young and old, male and female, powerful and powerless, all people of the earth shall praise the name of the Lord (v. 11–13).

These thirteen verses gather all heaven and earth in praise to God, a display of the future kingdom of God, fully and finally established. It has been promised to God's people (Isaiah 4:2–6; Jeremiah 23:5; Matthew 9:35), but its time has not yet come. As of now, we do not yet see everything in submission to him (Hebrews 2:8). God's name is not revered by the powerful and prestigious. But the psalmist interjects the person, the cornerstone, upon which this kingdom comes, even now.

Like the other Psalms of Praise, all are called to praise God for his name and his works (v. 13). His name is above all the heavens and the earth, which are prescribed to declare his glory. His nature is far superior to anything he has made. His work is the raising of a horn for the people (v. 14). The "horn" was ancient and symbolic language for the strong one, the king who would rule with power. Psalm 18:2 links such a strong king with the God who saves. *"The LORD is my rock and my fortress and my deliverer, my God, my rock, in whom I take refuge, my shield, and the horn of my salvation, my stronghold."* By the first century, near the time of Jesus's birth, the term "horn of salvation" meant the Messiah (Luke 1:69). When we recognize that God's most marvelous work—his salvation—is called a horn, we too can make that link.

Jesus, raised up on the cross to set the people free, became the mighty Savior. Jesus, raised into the heavens, became the king who would come with power and reign forever (Revelation 19:11–13, 16). When he first came, he set the children of God free from sin and brought eternal life through the Spirit. When he comes again, he will release all creation from bondage to decay and death. He will condemn and destroy all enemies to God. And death itself will be conquered by him. All the dead belonging to him will be raised to life. Then the end will come and Jesus, the horn of salvation, will hand over the kingdom to God the Father (1 Corinthians 15:24–28).

We wait for that day of fulfillment with great expectation. We wait with longing for mountains and hills to break forth in singing, for the trees of the field to clap their hands (Isaiah 55:12). We wait with hope for the sea to roar and the rivers to applaud this mighty king (Psalm 98:7–9). The song of the angels has already begun, and the horn has already been lifted up. It is time to take our part. Praise the Lord. Praise the Lord. Praise the Lord!

REFLECTION:

If trees can praise God by "clapping their hands" with the rattle of their shimmering leaves in the breeze, and if the sun can glorify God by its glittering light, what does that say about the way to praise God?

What is one way you can do that?

NOTES

NOTES

STUDY GUIDE

Using This Study

HOW TO GET THE MOST OUT OF THIS STUDY

As with any individual or small group study of God's Word, you largely reap what you sow. You get out of it what you put into it. Additionally, there are guidelines that can help you get the most from your efforts. Here are some suggestions to review before you get started.

1. Review the Table of Contents. The section entitled "Small Group Leader Helps" lays out best practices for how to host and facilitate a healthy small group and avoid common mistakes. It's a great idea to review this material before having your first meeting.

2. This book is a tool for facilitation. Adapt it to the needs of your group. If a line of discussion leads to green pastures outside the scope of the book, enjoy the leading of the Good Shepherd. Feel free to ask, or allow other members to ask, insightful questions as the Holy Spirit leads.

3. There is a lot of material here. You do not have to ask every question in your group discussion. Feel free to skip questions as needed and linger over the ones where there is authentic conversation.

4. Enjoy the experience. Christian community should be characterized by joy and love. Encourage yourself and the group members to bear such fruit. Pray before each session—ask God to minister to you, the facilitator, and every group member by name. Pray for the discussion, the fellowship, and the personal application.

5. Read the "Outline of Each Session" on the following pages so you understand the flow of the session and how the study works.

OUTLINE OF EACH SESSION

OPENING AND CLOSING PRAYER
Begin and end each session with prayer. Invite God into the midst of your conversation. Use the prayers provided or offer one of your own. The prayers provided could be offered by a member of the group or you could all say them together. Close your group with an offer to pray with one another. There is a prayer journal on page 202 where you can keep track of prayer requests and God's answers to your prayers.

KEY VERSE
Each session begins with a key verse. This verse is a key to understanding the entire week's theme. You may want to memorize these verses. By committing portions of God's Word to long-term memory, you can always refer to them, even when you don't have a Bible with you.

GETTING STARTED QUESTIONS
As you gather, a couple of questions are offered to help engage the topic and theme of the selected Scripture for the lesson. They also help build mutual trust with one another. Use the opening questions as an opportunity to reconnect each week and re-engage in the discussion.

ENCOUNTER THE WORD
PAYING ATTENTION TO THE TEXT AND MAKING OBSERVATIONS
The Scripture readings and video teachings serve as a unit to help you focus on the key ideas of the lesson, uncovering and developing God's promises in the assigned Scripture.

The initial questions under this section help group members make observations and interpret the text. Use as many or as few of these questions as proves helpful.

The video segment will provide teaching on the passage and direction for the session, serving as a launchpad for your discussion. You can watch this video ahead of the meeting as individuals, or if possible, watch it as a group. If you are hosting this group as an online group and are experiencing diminished quality, you may need to encourage members to take time to watch the video on their own rather than try to play it through your online meeting platform.

The "Video Notes" section offers summaries of key points or "Big Concepts" from the video teaching. You may want to ask the group a simple question after the video, something like: "What resonated with you from that video teaching?"

The "Study Notes" section provides space to take notes as you watch the video or hear inspirational thoughts from the Lord or members of your group.

ENGAGE OUR HEARTS
APPLYING SCRIPTURE TO DEVELOP INTIMACY WITH GOD
God's Word calls us to respond by being drawn into deeper trust of God. This section helps you to apply Scripture to your personal lives and to call you to greater intimacy and vulnerability with God.

ENCOURAGE OTHERS
BEARING WITNESS TO JESUS IN THE WORLD
Strengthened by God's Word, we can encourage and engage with our brothers and sisters in Christ, in a more meaningful and productive way. The questions in this section will invite you to apply what you are learning

Week 1
THE SON OF MAN
PSALM 8

OPENING PRAYER

Almighty and everlasting God, you made the universe with all its marvelous order, its atoms, worlds, and galaxies, and the infinite complexity of living creatures: Grant that, as we probe the mysteries of your creation, we may come to know you more truly, and more surely fulfill our role in your eternal purpose; in the name of Jesus Christ our Lord. *Amen.*

- Book of Common Prayer, p. 827

INTRODUCTION

Psalm 8 traces the great movement we have been exploring in the Creation Psalms, examining God in relation to his cosmic universe, as if we are looking through a telescope. In the devotions, we have considered the heavens—the planets, stars, and skies. We have tracked the formation of the earth—from the mountain peaks to caverns in the ocean depths. In Psalm 8, the field focuses, as if looking through a microscope, on the finite and fragile existence of humans, amplifying our importance. We have come to the pinnacle of God's creation—mankind.

In Psalm 8, we feel as if we have interloped upon a private setting, even a time of prayer, perhaps on a scenic hilltop in the Judean countryside. There we find David, the psalmist, contemplating the greatness of God. Inspired by his setting, and perhaps his own personal concerns for his future, David—the shepherd and king—speculates on mankind's role in God's great universe. Through this prayerful inquiry, God casts a vision for the unique and exalted calling for mankind. Like other elements of God's created order, we are meant to reflect God's glory. But embedded into this Scripture is also God's provision that enables us to fulfill our calling—namely Jesus Christ. Psalm 8 is a beautiful reflection on the correlation of God and mankind, his vision for our lives, and his plan to teach us how to be fully alive.

KEY VERSE

"What is man that you are mindful of him, and the son of man that you care for him?"

PSALM 8:4

GETTING STARTED

What are some of the great achievements of humanity?

What are some of the greatest failures of humanity?

ENCOUNTER THE WORD

PAYING ATTENTION TO THE TEXT AND MAKING OBSERVATIONS

Read Psalm 8.
1. While David is evidently stargazing and meditating on the vastness and brilliance of God's creation in verses 1–3, what is his big, cosmic question in verse 4?

2. What are indications that humankind holds a special place in creation (v. 5–8)? In what way is this designation a noble or royal calling?

Note: The Hebrew the word for "glory" can mean "weight, importance, or worthiness."

3. What attributes of man in this passage reflect the character of God? (You might want to consider some of the traits we encountered in the Creation Psalms.)

....

WATCH VIDEO

The video teaching can be found at **biblestudymedia.com/pilgrimspath**.

Video Notes

BIG CONCEPTS:

- Mankind's calling is royal and comes with sovereignty.
- The fall of mankind—the loss of dominion and the crown
- Jesus fulfills the calling of mankind.
- God accomplishes his plan for humanity through his Son, Jesus.

ENGAGE OUR HEARTS

APPLYING SCRIPTURE TO DEVELOP INTIMACY WITH GOD

4. In what ways are we unable to fulfill God's calling to humanity on our own?

    a) What is not under our power or dominion?

    b) What things tarnish our crown or diminish the glory God had in mind for us?

5. How was God "mindful" of us when he sent Jesus (the Son of Man—Jesus's favorite title for himself) to walk in our humanity?

6. What character trait(s) would you assign to God, based on his plan of salvation enacted through Jesus, his Son? (See also 1 John 4:9–10.)

7. Irenaeus, the early church father and theologian said, "The glory of God is man fully alive." The disciple John said we have seen God's glory in his Son Jesus (John 1:14). What does that mean for us? (See also John 17:22–23.)

> *Jesus said, "I came that they might have life and have it abundantly."*
>
> **JOHN 10:10**

ENCOURAGE OTHERS

BEARING WITNESS TO JESUS IN THE WORLD

8. Is there someone you know who needs to be "crowned" with glory (using the definition in **Note** after question 2)? What are ways that you can esteem others that will help them remember their divine, royal calling?

9. Jesus acted completely under the authority of God while he walked on earth, and yet he had authority over everything. In what capacity do you have dominion or authority (family, work, community)? Are there any issues that need to be more fully submitted to God's authority? How can you do that? What do you think will be the outcome?

10. When Jesus wore his crown on earth, he lay down his life for others. Is there someone you need to forgive or bear their burden? Is there something (a behavior, an attitude) you may need to set aside or sacrifice in order that another may live more fully?

PRAYERS

If you are doing this study as part of a group, you may want to share your prayer requests with each other. There is a Prayer & Praise Journal on p. 202 where you can keep track of your group's requests or write your own. Have someone close in prayer or pray the following prayer together.

CLOSING PRAYER

O God, who wonderfully created, and yet more wonderfully restored, the dignity of human nature: Grant that we may share the divine life of him who humbled himself to share our humanity, your Son Jesus Christ, who lives and reigns with you, in the unity of the Holy Spirit, one God, for ever and ever. *Amen.*

- Book of Common Prayer, p. 214

Week 2
THE KING OF GLORY
PSALM 24

OPENING PRAYER

O God, by your grace, help us to understand your truth as presented in your holy Word, and most fully revealed in your Son, Jesus Christ. Grant that by the study of your Word, we would know you as the one true God and love you with our whole heart, through the indwelling grace and power of your Son, Jesus our Lord. In his name we pray, *Amen.*

INTRODUCTION

Psalm 24 is the culmination of our lesson on three types of psalms: Torah Psalms (or psalms about God's Word/law), Wisdom Psalms, and Psalms of Well-Being. It ties together the elements we have been learning in our devotions, namely that God's law provides the guide to righteousness, by which we may come to know and love God more fully. It is fitting then that Psalm 24 opens with David reflecting on God's holiness and how to draw near to him in worship. The psalm recounts the event when David brought the ark of the covenant into the city of Jerusalem, often referred to as Mt. Zion. David reflects on the character required to enter the presence of God. Remarkably, however, he also depicts the character of the One who entered our presence so that such a union would be possible at all.

KEY VERSE

"Who is this King of glory? The LORD, strong and mighty, the LORD, mighty in battle! Lift up your heads, O gates! And lift them up, O ancient doors, that the King of glory may come in."

PSALM 24:8–9

....

GETTING STARTED

Have you ever given up on a New Year's resolution, diet, exercise routine, or commitment to a healthier life pattern? Why do you think you gave up? What would have helped you to keep your commitment?

....

ENCOUNTER THE WORD

PAYING ATTENTION TO THE TEXT AND MAKING OBSERVATIONS

Read Psalm 24.

1. Psalm 24 is essentially a processional hymn, commemorating the entrance of the ark of the covenant into Jerusalem (See 2 Samuel 6:12–17). For whom or what are the congregants/worshippers preparing in verses 7–10? Where did they believe his presence dwelled (See also Exodus 25:10–22)?

2. The question of *"ascending the hill"* and *"standing in his holy place"* (v. 3) is a question about entering the Lord's presence in worship. What are the criteria to enter the Lord's presence, according to the psalm? In what way is this list similar to the Ten Commandments?

3. Who is the King of Glory, according to the psalm, and what are his attributes?

WATCH VIDEO

The video teaching can be found at **biblestudymedia.com/pilgrimspath**.

Video Notes

BIG CONCEPTS:

- God's holiness and the criteria to enter God's presence
- God's law is a law of love—learning and living the character of God.
- The King of Glory
- A new way to worship, a new way to enter his presence

....

ENGAGE OUR HEARTS

APPLYING SCRIPTURE TO DEVELOP INTIMACY WITH GOD

4. What does Jesus say in John 5:17? Why is this good news for us (Romans 7:15–25)?

5. In what ways is Jesus a warrior, victor, and conqueror for us? (See 1 Corinthians 15:54–57 and Revelation 19:11–16.) Review Psalm 24:4–5. Is there a specific area where you need Jesus to battle on your behalf? Write a prayer here with that specific request.

6. What does Hebrews 10:14 say is happening to us who believe in Jesus and his work on the cross? Therefore, what can we do, according to Hebrews 10:19?

ENCOURAGE OTHERS

BEARING WITNESS TO JESUS IN THE WORLD

7. What does Jesus say is our reward for obeying his commands (John 14:21, 23)?

8. How does the knowledge of Jesus's righteousness <u>in you</u> change how you view yourself? How does it change your ability to:

    - love those difficult to love?
    - forgive those difficult to forgive?
    - persevere in difficult circumstances?

    Feel free to add to this list of things you can do with Jesus.

9. Is there someone you would like to invite into this procession? What would you tell them awaits?

....

PRAYERS

If you are doing this study as part of a group, you may want to share your prayer requests with each other. There is a Prayer & Praise Journal on p. 202 where you can keep track of your group's requests or write your own. Have someone close in prayer or pray the following prayer together.

CLOSING PRAYER

O God, who in love and pity sent us Jesus Christ to be the Light in our darkness, give me wisdom to profit from the words he spoke, and grace to follow in his footsteps.

Jesus said: *Whenever you stand praying, forgive, if you have anything against anyone; so that your Father in heaven may also forgive you all your trespasses.*

>O God, give me the grace to do this now.

Jesus said: *It is more blessed to give than to receive.*

>O God, give me grace today not to think of what I can get, but of what I can give.

Jesus said: *When you give alms, do not let your left hand know what your right hand is doing.*

>O God, grant that what I give may be given without self-satisfaction and without thought of praise or reward.

Jesus said: *Enter through the narrow gate.*

>O God, give me grace today to keep to the narrow path of duty and honest dealing.

Jesus said: *Do not judge.*

>O God, give me grace today to take the plank out of my own eye before I look at the speck in my brother's or sister's eye.

Jesus said: *What good is it for someone to gain the whole world, yet lose their own soul?*

>O God, give me grace to live this day in such a way that whatever else I lose, I will not lose my soul, my very life in you.

Amen.

- Excerpt from John Baillie's "A Diary of Private Prayer," Eighth Day, Morning.[34]

Week 3
THREADS OF FAITH
PSALM 137

OPENING PRAYER

Lord God of hosts, set my experience of present trouble firmly in the structure of your great acts of salvation. And then help me to believe that your way is being worked out even in the chaos of this world I live in, through Jesus Christ. *Amen.*[35]

INTRODUCTION

Psalm 137 is perhaps the most desperate and hateful psalm in the Psalter, compiling the unruly emotions, complaints, and fears of the Psalms of Lament. The psalm is set in the context of the Babylonian exile, after the destruction of the temple in Jerusalem. The psalmist and his companions weep and mourn for the loss of everything—their homeland, their culture, their center of worship, and, conceivably, their God. The psalm seethes with loss, bitterness, and hate. And yet, in its painful honesty and vulnerability, it reveals a faith that clings to God, who is still there.

Psalm 137 is an unlikely model of prayer for us in our times of greatest need. In it we discover that our faith has matured from a polite religiosity to an unshakeable conviction girded to God in a new way. During these difficult times, we can experience a greater intimacy with God, even the fellowship of sharing in the suffering of his Son, Jesus Christ. He is with us, he knows our pain, and he will sustain us while we wait for God to make all things right. Even if we cannot yet *"sing in a foreign land"* (v. 4), we can at least pray.

KEY VERSE

"How shall we sing the LORD's song in a foreign land?"

PSALM 137:4

GETTING STARTED

Can you remember a time when you thought God had abandoned you? What were the circumstances? What did you learn as you walked through that time?

ENCOUNTER THE WORD

PAYING ATTENTION TO THE TEXT AND MAKING OBSERVATIONS

Read Psalm 137.

1. Why are the people weeping in verses 1–3? (See Psalm 74 and 79 for context.)

2. What/who are they afraid they will forget (v. 4–6)?

3. What do they want God to remember and to do?

WATCH VIDEO

The video teaching can be found at **biblestudymedia.com/pilgrimspath**.

Video Notes

BIG CONCEPTS:

- A new way of prayer
- A new intimacy with God
- Our suffering has a purpose.

....

ENGAGE OUR HEARTS

APPLYING SCRIPTURE TO DEVELOP INTIMACY WITH GOD

4. According to Hebrews 4:14–16, why is it safe to pour out our most difficult emotions in prayer to Jesus? (See also Psalm 139 and John 10:14.)

5. According to Romans 8:26, how can God help us pray in our deepest grief? What do you think he prays for?

6. What part of Jesus's suffering do you understand better, having been through it yourself? What part of your suffering do you think he understands having been through it himself?

ENCOURAGE OTHERS

BEARING WITNESS TO JESUS IN THE WORLD

7. How can God use your time of grief to bless another in theirs? (See 2 Corinthians 1:3–6.)

8. What aspects of this lesson give you confidence or courage to walk by someone's side in grief?

PRAYERS

If you are doing this study as part of a group, you may want to share your prayer requests with each other. There is a Prayer & Praise Journal on p. 202 where you can keep track of your group's requests or write your own. Have someone close in prayer or pray the following prayer together.

CLOSING PRAYER

I am so used to hiding my feelings and thoughts that others might find unacceptable, O God, that I even try to do it with you. Keep me honest in my prayers. You know how to deal with such as me: I do not fear your rejection, and I hope in your salvation, even in Jesus Christ. *Amen.*[36]

NOTES

Week 4
GRACIOUS FORGIVENESS
PSALM 32

OPENING PRAYER

Almighty God, you who have sent Jesus into the world to suffer, die, and rise again for our sake, help us to experience your transforming resurrection power within our lives and ministry. We offer our prayers in the name and Spirit of Jesus Christ, our Lord. *Amen.*[37]

INTRODUCTION

Psalm 32 is an excellent summary of the Psalms of Internal Lament, covered in Week 4 of our devotions. It leads us through the vital movement of confessing our sins, accepting the gift of forgiveness as an act of sheer grace from God, and walking into the new life he calls us. In an interesting play on words, Psalm 32 shows us the essential elements of the law of grace, where our faith is counted as righteousness. Through Christ, we find that our transgressions are taken off, our sins are covered, and we are clothed in his righteousness. Though Psalm 32 is still a lament, we can join the psalmist in shouts of joy as we understand what Jesus has done for us.

KEY VERSE

"Blessed is the one whose transgression is forgiven, whose sin is covered."

PSALM 32:1

GETTING STARTED

Can you think of a time when you were glad to "come clean" in a relationship (when you revealed the truth about your feelings or behavior, past or present)? In your experience, what happens to a relationship that is based on truth, no matter how painful?

ENCOUNTER THE WORD

PAYING ATTENTION TO THE TEXT AND MAKING OBSERVATIONS

Read Psalm 32.

1. David, the psalmist, starts with his conclusion. Who is the one who lives a happy, fulfilled life (v. 1–2)?

2. What does God not count according to verse 2? What does he count, according to Romans 4:3–5?

3. Describe David's state of mind and body when he harbored his guilt (v. 3–4). Do you think sin and guilt have a physical impact on the body? If so, in what ways?

4. Compare verse 4 with verse 7. What has happened to David's relationship with God as a result of confessing his sins and being forgiven?

WATCH VIDEO

The video teaching can be found at **biblestudymedia.com/pilgrimspath**.

Video Notes

BIG CONCEPTS:

- The movement from guilt to forgiveness
- Understanding our predicament: rebels and sinners by birth
- God's gracious act of imputing righteousness
- Our responsibility—clothed in power

ENGAGE OUR HEARTS

APPLYING SCRIPTURE TO DEVELOP INTIMACY WITH GOD

5. In what ways does sin feel "heavy" upon you? Why do you think this is so? (Consider Romans 2:5.)

6. What does it require on your part to confess your sins to God? (See v. 2b and Psalm 51:6.) Why is this so hard to do sometimes?

7. According to verse 5, what do we have to do to receive God's forgiveness? (See also Acts 2:38; Acts 10:43.) Describe what this grace means to you.

ENCOURAGE OTHERS

BEARING WITNESS TO JESUS IN THE WORLD

8. If God has not counted your sins against you and this same grace applies to all believers, how does this understanding affect your response to others when they sin against you or God? (See Colossians 3:12–13; John 13:14–17.)

9. How can we forgive even after the worst offenses against us (v. 8; Acts 1:8; John 16:12–15)?

10. How might your forgiveness of others be a witness to Jesus in the world?

....

PRAYERS

If you are doing this study as part of a group, you may want to share your prayer requests with each other. There is a Prayer & Praise Journal on p. 202 where you can keep track of your group's requests or write your own. Have someone close in prayer or pray the following prayer together.

CLOSING PRAYER

Loving God, clothe me in yourself and enable me to live and serve after the pattern of Jesus. Amen.[38]

NOTES

Week 5
THY KINGDOM COME
PSALM 98

OPENING PRAYER

Almighty and everlasting God, whose will it is to restore all things in your well-beloved Son, the King of kings and Lord of lords: Mercifully grant that the peoples of the earth, divided and enslaved by sin, may be freed and brought together under his most gracious rule; who lives and reigns with you and the Holy Spirit, one God, now and forever. *Amen.*

- Book of Common Prayer, p. 236

INTRODUCTION

Psalm 98 celebrates the coming of a new kingdom, ruled by a holy king who is also a righteous judge. His kingdom will rule over all the earth for all people, races, and nations. The crowning achievement for this rule will be a salvation that restores all creation to its intended state—free, joyous, and in perfect relationship with a loving, faithful God. Psalm 98 is a prophetic picture of the coming of Jesus to first-century Judea and Palestine and his triumphant return at the end of time.

KEY VERSE

"Oh sing to the LORD a new song, for he has done marvelous things!"

PSALM 98:1

....

GETTING STARTED

Have you ever attended a great celebration event—a wedding, an ordination of a minister or priest, or an inauguration of a president? What elements characterized that event? How do these ceremonies proclaim that something new is happening or that there is a status change?

....

ENCOUNTER THE WORD

PAYING ATTENTION TO THE TEXT AND MAKING OBSERVATIONS

Read Psalm 98.

1. Based on verse 1, what is the most marvelous thing God has done?

2. If the Lord is king (v. 6), what kind of rule does he establish, and where?

3. This king is also a judge (v. 9) who judges the whole earth—the world and its peoples. Describe the response to his judgment as exhibited throughout the psalm. Why do you think the recipients of judgment respond this way?

4. Who praises the Lord in this psalm?

WATCH VIDEO

The video teaching can be found at **biblestudymedia.com/pilgrimspath**.

Video Notes

BIG CONCEPTS:

- Heralding a new kingdom
- The right hand and holy arm save.
- The Holy Savior is the king.
- The king will judge the earth.
- The coming kingdom under Jesus

....

ENGAGE OUR HEARTS

APPLYING SCRIPTURE TO DEVELOP INTIMACY WITH GOD

5. Verse 1 tells us that God's right hand and his holy arm have worked salvation. He alone has done this. What does his single-handed power suggest to you? (See also Isaiah 59:1,16.)

6. Why, in your opinion, did God work salvation for the world (v. 1–3)?

7. If you were telling someone else about the salvation of Jesus, what would you tell them about salvation based on the following Scriptures? (If you are in a group, you may want to divide these Scriptures among you.)

    John 2:1–11
    John 4:1–30
    John 5:1–9
    John 9:1–7
    John 11:1–43

    How do these scenes help answer question 6, in part?

8. In what ways was Jesus's salvation and righteousness made known to the world (v. 2)?

   Here are a few of the ways. (Feel free to pick and choose, look them all up, or add more.)

   Matthew 2:9–12
   John 3:22
   John 10:23–25
   Luke 12:1
   John 18:20
   John 19:19–22
   Acts 2:1–14, 22–24
   Acts 26:25–29

   As Paul said in Acts 26:25–29, God's salvation has not been accomplished in a corner. Why is it important to know this was done for everyone, everywhere?

9. What impact will the open, public knowledge of salvation in Jesus have on judgment day? (See John 9:35–41 and John 10:22–26.)

10 Have you found God's salvation in Jesus? If not, would you like to pray now for God to reveal it to you in an obvious way?

ENCOURAGE OTHERS

BEARING WITNESS TO JESUS IN THE WORLD

11. How would this psalm be an effective advertisement to others who do not know the Lord?

12. Describe the reason for so much joy in this psalm.

PRAYERS

If you are doing this study as part of a group, you may want to share your prayer requests with each other. There is a Prayer & Praise Journal on p. 202 where you can keep track of your group's requests or write your own. Have someone close in prayer or pray the following prayer together.

CLOSING PRAYER

"Our Father in heaven,
hallowed be your name.
Your kingdom come,
your will be done,
on earth as it is in heaven.
Give us this day our daily bread,
and forgive us our debts,
as we also have forgiven our debtors.
And lead us not into temptation,
but deliver us from evil.
For yours is the kingdom
and the power
and the glory, forever.
Amen."

MATTHEW 6:9–13

Week 6
UNENDING PRAISE
PSALM 150

OPENING PRAYER

Heavenly Father, you have filled the world with beauty: open our eyes to recognize your gracious hand in all your works; that we may rejoice with all your creation and learn to serve you with complete gladness, for the sake of your Son, Jesus Christ, through whom all things were made. *Amen.*

- Book of Common Prayer, p. 814, *adapted*

INTRODUCTION

As we come to the last psalm of the Psalter and of this study, we experience something like a grand finale, with clashing cymbals, blaring trumpets, and shimmering tambourines—a festival of sorts. One might expect a display of fireworks at the end. If the psalmist has only one thing to say at the close of this collection of poems, prayers, and songs, Psalm 150 is it. The psalmist concludes that our life is meant for praise. All of creation was designed to join in unison to praise God, revealing his glory as seen in his mighty deeds and his excellent greatness. When we praise God, we become the outward expression of his glory. Joy is the outcome of our life of praise and the expression of our lives. Hallelujah! Praise the Lord.

KEY VERSE

"Let everything that has breath praise the LORD."

PSALM 150:6

GETTING STARTED

Eugene Peterson said, "All prayer, pursued far enough, becomes praise."[39] Can you remember a time when praying changed your attitude, even while you prayed? Why do you think that happens?

ENCOUNTER THE WORD

PAYING ATTENTION TO THE TEXT AND MAKING OBSERVATIONS

Read Psalm 150.

1. The psalmist summons us to praise God in his sanctuary. According to our study, where is God's sanctuary? (See Psalm 29; Psalm 27:4–6; Psalm 23:5–6; John 1:14; Ephesians 2:22.)

2. According to verse 2, what are the two main things for which we praise God? What are some things that fall under these two categories, as expressed in Psalm 103?

3. How should we praise God, according to verses 3–5? What strikes you about these verses?

4. Who is called to praise the Lord in verse 6? Based on our study, what/who else might this include besides people? (See also Psalm 148:7–10; 103:20–22.)

WATCH VIDEO

The video teaching can be found at **biblestudymedia.com/pilgrimspath**.

Video Notes

BIG CONCEPTS:

- We are to praise God everywhere, at all times.
- Praise acknowledges God's powerful works and righteous loving character.
- Praise is an intentional, external expression.
- Praise changes us by an "expansion" of God's Spirit in us.
- Praise produces joy in us and in others.
- Praise is for everyone.

ENGAGE OUR HEARTS

APPLYING SCRIPTURE TO DEVELOP INTIMACY WITH GOD

5. Why can we praise God even in hardship and suffering? Have you ever done this? How did it impact you?

6. When we praise God, we align ourselves with him, with his Spirit. What is the gift we receive according to Galatians 5:22–23? How does this change the way we pray?

7. What happens, in your opinion, when you align your prayers with God's will?

ENCOURAGE OTHERS

BEARING WITNESS TO JESUS IN THE WORLD

8. How can we praise God with our whole being?

9. How does our praise reflect his glory to others?

10. If we experience joy when we praise, and we are to praise God continually, what does that mean for our daily attitude and experience? How are we to live? What does this say about God?

11. Do you think the world understands the concept of God's joy? How could we change their concept of God?

....

PRAYERS

If you are doing this study as part of a group, you may want to share your prayer requests with each other. There is a Prayer & Praise Journal on p. 202 where you can keep track of your group's requests or write your own. Have someone close in prayer or pray the following prayer together.

CLOSING PRAYER

Praise, my soul, the King of heaven;
to his feet your tribute bring.
Ransomed, healed, restored, forgiven,
evermore his praises sing.
Alleluia, alleluia!
Praise the everlasting King!

Praise him for his grace and favor
to his people in distress.
Praise him, still the same as ever,
slow to chide, and swift to bless.
Alleluia, alleluia!
Glorious in his faithfulness!

Fatherlike he tends and spares us;
well our feeble frame he knows.
In his hand he gently bears us,
rescues us from all our foes.
Alleluia, alleluia!
Widely yet his mercy flows!

Angels, help us to adore him;
you behold him face to face.
Sun and moon, bow down before him,
dwellers all in time and space.
Alleluia, alleluia!
Praise with us the God of grace![40]

END NOTES

Introduction

[1] Timothy Keller and Kathy Keller, *The Songs of Jesus, A Year of Daily Devotions in the Psalms* (New York: Viking, 2015), viii.

[2] Even longer for some of the psalms. Psalm 90 is attributed to Moses, possibly dating to the fourteenth century BC.

[3] Eugene Peterson, *Answering God* (New York: Harper Collins, 1989), 127.

[4] John Stott, *Favorite Psalms* (Chicago: Moody Press, 1988), 5.

[5] Walter Brueggemann, *The Message of the Psalms, A Theological Commentary* (Minneapolis, MN: Augsburg, 1984). —The grouping of psalms in this study and the pattern they represent in our faith life is based in part on Walter Brueggemann's idea of orientation, disorientation and reorientation to God in his commentary.

Week 1

[6] As Keller points out, by the order and boundaries set into creation, we can understand the principles of science—mathematics, physics, chemistry, and biology, and all the industry that flows out of those (*The Songs of Jesus*, p. 258). But we can also understand and engage in art, including architecture, painting, sculpture, and music.

[7] "O mighty ones" could mean angels as in Psalm 89:6 and Job 1:6. Or it could also mean kings and rulers of nations.

[8] The Book of Common Prayer, The Episcopal Church (Church Publishing Incorporated, NY), 362.

[9] The Hebrew word *ruach* means breath or spirit or wind.

[10] Brueggemann, *The Message of the Psalms*, 34.

[11] Initially Israel, God's chosen people, but now also the people redeemed by Jesus Christ—the fulfillment of God's calling to Israel.

Week 2

[12] See also John 14:21–23.

[13] Charles Spurgeon, *Psalms, Volume II, The Crossway Classic Commentaries*, edited by Alister McGrath and J.I. Packer (Wheaton, IL: Crossway Books, 1993), 138.

[14] Charles Spurgeon, *Psalms, Volume I, The Crossway Classic Commentaries*, edited by Alister McGrath and J.I. Packer (Wheaton, IL: Crossway Books, 1993), 40.

[15] 1 Samuel 5:1–6; 6:19-20, 2 Samuel 6:3-9.

[16] Spurgeon, *Psalms, Volume I*, 42.

[17] Brueggemann, *The Message of the Psalms*, 48.

Week 3
[18] Spurgeon, *Psalms, Volume I*, 316.
[19] Edited by Brian Kolodiejchuk, M.C., *Mother Teresa Come Be My Light, The Private Writings of the Saint of Calcutta* (New York: Doubleday, 2007).
[20] Excerpts from *The Dark Night of the Soul*, edited by Richard J. Foster and James Bryan Smith, *Devotional Classics* (New York: HarperCollins, 1993), 33-37.

Week 4
[21] "The sacraments are outward and visible signs of inward and spiritual grace, given by Christ as sure and certain means by which we receive that grace." *The Book of Common Prayer* (New York: Church Publishing Incorporated, 2007), 857.
[22] God is consistently "for us." He is biased in his desires for things to work out for us (Romans 8:31).
[23] Webster's Ninth New Collegiate Dictionary (Springfield, MA: Merriam-Webster Inc, 1990), 986.

Week 5
[24] Brueggemann, *The Message of the Psalms*, 111.
[25] Keller, *The Songs of Jesus*, 294.
[26] Ibid.
[27] Brueggemann, *The Message of the Psalms*, 144.
[28] Ibid., 148.

Week 6
[29] Brueggemann, *The Message of the Psalms*, 158.
[30] Peterson, *Answering God*, 127.
[31] C. S. Lewis, *Reflections on the Psalms* (New York: HarperCollins, 1986), 109.
[32] C. S. Lewis said, "Praise is the consummation of our enjoyment of God." (*Reflections on the Psalms*, 111.) I think this is the same idea.
[33] Spurgeon, *Psalms, Volume II*, 365.

Study Guide
[34] John Baillie, *A Diary of Private Prayer*, updated and revised by Susanna Wright; (New York: Scribner, 2014), 31.
[35] Eugene H. Peterson, *Praying with the Psalms*, (New York: Harper One, 1993), June 5.
[36] Ibid., May 5.
[37] Rueben P. Job and Norman Shawchuck, *A Guide to Prayer for Ministers and Other Servants* (Nashville, TN: The Upper Room, 1983), 142.
[38] Ibid., 202.
[39] Peterson, *Answering God*, 127.
[40] Henry Francis Lyte, "Praise, My Soul, the King of Heaven," The Hymnal 1982 (New York: The Church Hymnal Corporation, 1985), 410.

Appendices

Prepared by Bible Study Media

FREQUENTLY ASKED QUESTIONS

WHAT DO WE DO ON THE FIRST NIGHT OF OUR GROUP?

Have a party! A "get to know you" coffee, dinner, or dessert is a great way to launch a new study. You may want to review the Small Group Covenant (p. 199) and share the names of a few friends you can invite to join you. But most importantly, have fun before your study time begins.

WHERE DO WE FIND NEW MEMBERS FOR OUR GROUP?

Finding members can be troubling, especially for new groups that have only a few people or for existing groups that have lost a few people along the way. We encourage you to pray with your group and then brainstorm a list of people from work, church, your neighborhood, your children's school, family, the gym, and so forth. Use the five circles on page 198 to identify potential group members with whom you would like to build a spiritual friendship. Have each group member invite several people on his or her list.

No matter how you find members, it is vital that you stay on the lookout for new people to join your group. All groups tend to go through healthy attrition—the result of moves, sending out new leaders, ministry opportunities, and so forth—and if the group gets too small, it could be at risk of ending. If you and your group stay open to ideas, you will be amazed at the people God sends your way. The next person just might become a friend for life.

HOW LONG WILL THIS GROUP MEET?

Most groups meet weekly for at least their first 6 weeks, but every other week can work as well. We strongly recommend that the group meet for the first 6 months on a weekly basis if possible. This allows for continuity and, if people miss a meeting, they aren't gone for a whole month.

At the end of this study, each group member may decide if he or she wants to continue for another study. Some groups launch relationships for years to come, and others are steppingstones into another group experience. Either way, enjoy the journey.

CAN WE DO THIS STUDY ON OUR OWN?

Absolutely! One of the best ways to do this study is not with a full house but with a few friends. You may choose to gather with another couple who would enjoy some relational time (perhaps going to the movies or having a quiet dinner) and then walking through this six-week study. Jesus will be with you even if there are only two of you (Matthew 18:20).

WHAT IF THIS GROUP IS NOT WORKING FOR US?

You're not alone! This could be the result of a personality conflict, life stage difference, geographical distance, level of spiritual maturity, or any number of things. Relax. Pray for God's direction, and at the end of this six-week study, decide whether to continue with this group or find another. You don't typically buy the first car you test drive or marry the first person you date, and the same goes with a group. However, don't give up before the six weeks are up—God might have something to teach you. Also, don't run from conflict or prejudge people before you have given them a chance. God is still working in your life, too!

WHO IS THE LEADER?

Most groups have an official leader. But ideally, the group will mature, and members will rotate the leadership of meetings. We have discovered that healthy groups rotate hosts/leaders and homes on a regular basis. This model ensures that all members grow, make their unique contribution, and develop their gifts. This study guide and the Holy Spirit can keep things on track even when you rotate leaders. Christ has promised to be in your midst as you gather. Ultimately, God is your leader each step of the way.

HOW DO WE HANDLE THE CHILDCARE NEEDS IN OUR GROUP?

Very carefully. This can be a sensitive issue. We suggest that you empower the group to openly brainstorm solutions. You may try one option that works for a while and then adjust over time. Our favorite approach is for adults to meet in the living room or dining room and to share the cost of a babysitter (or two) who can watch the children in a different part of the house. This way, parents don't have to be away from their children all evening when their children are too young to be left at home. A second option is to use one home for the children and a second home (close by or a phone call away) for the adults. A third idea is to rotate the responsibility of providing a lesson or care for the children either in the same home or in another home nearby. This can be an incredible blessing for young ones. Finally, the most common solution is to decide that you need to have a night to invest in your spiritual lives individually or as a couple and to make your own arrangements for childcare. No matter what decision the group makes, the best approach is to dialogue openly about both the need and the solution.

CIRCLES OF LIFE

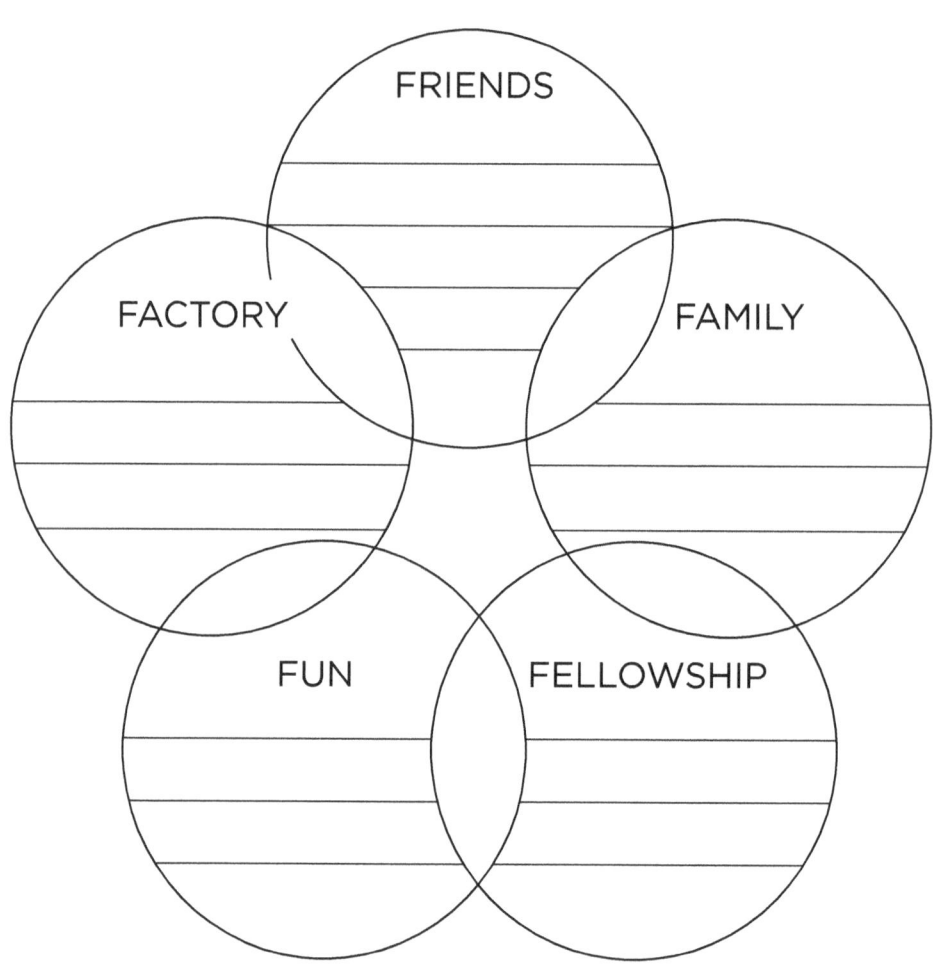

SMALL GROUP COVENANT

OUR PURPOSE
To provide a predictable environment where participants experience authentic Christian community to grow spiritually.

GROUP ATTENDANCE
To give priority to the group meeting. We will call or email if we will be late or absent. (Completing the Group Calendar on p. 200 will minimize this issue.)

SAFE ENVIRONMENT
To help create a safe place where people can be heard and feel loved. (Please, no quick answers, snap judgments, or simple fixes.)

RESPECT DIFFERENCES
To be gentle and gracious with different spiritual maturity levels, personal opinions, temperaments, or "imperfections" in fellow group members. We are all works in progress.

CONFIDENTIALITY
To keep anything that is shared strictly confidential and within the group, and to avoid sharing improper information about those outside the group.

ENCOURAGEMENT FOR GROWTH
To be not just takers, but givers of life. We want to spiritually multiply our lives by serving others with our God-given gifts.

SHARED OWNERSHIP
To remember that every member is a minister and to ensure that each attender will share a small team role or responsibility over time.

ROTATING HOSTS, FACILITATORS, AND HOMES
To encourage different people to host the group in their homes and to rotate the responsibility of facilitating each meeting. (See the Group Calendar on p. 200.)

SMALL GROUP CALENDAR

Planning and calendaring can help ensure the greatest participation at every meeting. At the end of each meeting, review this calendar. Be sure to include a regular rotation of host homes and facilitator, and don't forget birthdays, socials, church events, holidays, and mission/ministry projects.

DATE	SESSION	HOST HOME

SNACKS	FACILITATOR

PRAYER & PRAISE JOURNAL

1

2

3

4

5

6

SMALL GROUP ROSTER

NAME	EMAIL	CELL PHONE

SMALL GROUP LEADER HELPS

HOSTING AN OPEN HOUSE

If you're starting a new group, try planning an Open House before your first formal group meeting. Even if you have only two to four core members, it's a great way to break the ice and prayerfully consider who else might be open to joining you over the next few weeks. You can also use this kick-off meeting to hand out books, spend some time getting to know each other, discuss each person's expectations for the group, and briefly pray for each other. A simple meal or good dessert always make a kickoff meeting more fun. After people introduce themselves and share how they ended up being at the meeting (you can play a game to see who has the wildest story!), have everyone respond to a few icebreaker questions, such as:

- What is your favorite family vacation?
- What is one thing you love about your church/our community?
- What are two things about your life growing up that most people here don't know?

Next, ask everyone to tell what he or she hopes to get out of the study. You might want to review the Small Group Covenant on p. _ and talk about each person's expectations and priorities. Finally, set an open chair (maybe two) in the center of your group and explain that it represents someone who would enjoy or benefit from this group who isn't here yet.

Ask people to pray about inviting someone to join the group over the next few weeks. Hand out postcards and have everyone write an invitation or two. Don't worry about ending up with too many people; you can always have one discussion circle in the living room and another in the dining room after you watch the lesson. Each group could then report prayer requests and progress at the end of the session.

You can skip this kickoff meeting if your time is limited, but you'll experience a huge benefit if you take the time to connect with one another in this way.

LEADING FOR THE FIRST TIME

SEVEN COMMON LEADERSHIP EXPERIENCES.
WELCOME TO LIFE OUT IN FRONT!

Sweaty palms are a healthy sign. The Bible says God is gracious to the humble. Remember who is in control; the time to worry is when you're not worried. Those who are soft in heart (and sweaty-palmed) are those whom God is sure to speak through.

Seek support. Ask your leader, co-leader, or a close friend to pray for you and prepare with you before the session. Walking through the study will help you anticipate potentially difficult questions and discussion topics.

Bring your uniqueness to the study. Lean into who you are and how God wants you to uniquely lead the study.

Prepare. Prepare. Prepare. Go through the session, read the section of Scripture. If you are using the video, listen to the teaching segment. Consider writing in a journal or praying through the day to prepare yourself for what God wants to do. Don't wait until the last minute to prepare.

Ask for feedback so you can grow. Perhaps in an email or on index cards handed out at the study, have everyone write down three things you did well and one thing you could improve on. Don't get defensive. Instead, show an openness to learn and grow.

Share with your group what God is doing in your heart. God is searching for those whose hearts are fully his. Share your trials and victories. We promise that people will relate.

Prayerfully consider whom you would like to pass the baton to next week. It's only fair. God is ready for the next member of your group to go on the faith journey you just traveled. Make it fun and expect God to do the rest.

LEADERSHIP TRAINING 101

Congratulations! You have responded to the call to help shepherd Jesus's flock. There are few other tasks in the family of God that surpass the contribution you will be making. As you prepare to lead, whether it is one session or the entire series, here are a few thoughts to keep in mind. We encourage you to read these and review them with each new discussion leader before he or she leads.

1. Remember that you are not alone. God knows everything about you, and he knew that you would be asked to lead this group. Remember that it is common for all good leaders to feel that they are not ready to lead. Moses, Solomon, Jeremiah, and Timothy were all reluctant to lead. God promises, *"Never will I leave you; never will I forsake you"* (Hebrews 13:5). Whether you are leading for one evening, for several weeks, or for a lifetime, you will be blessed as you serve.

2. Don't try to do it alone. Pray right now for God to help you build a healthy leadership team. If you can enlist a co-leader to help you lead the group, you will find your experience to be much richer. This is your chance to involve as many people as you can in building a healthy group. All you have to do is call and ask people to help. You'll probably be surprised at the response.

3. Just be yourself. If you won't be you, who will? God wants you to use your unique gifts and temperament. Don't try to do things exactly like another leader; do them in a way that fits you! Just admit it when you don't have an answer and apologize when you make a mistake. Your group will love you for it, and you'll sleep better at night!

4. Prepare for your meeting ahead of time. Review the session and write down your responses to each question. Pay special attention to exercises that ask group members to do something other than engage in discussion, like take an action. These exercises will help your group live what the Bible teaches, not just talk about it.

5. Pray for your group members by name. Before you begin your session, go around the room in your mind and pray for each member. Ask God to use your time together to touch the heart of every person uniquely. Expect God to lead you to whomever he wants you to encourage or

challenge in a special way. If you listen, God will surely lead!

6. When you ask a question, be patient. Someone will eventually respond. Sometimes people need a moment or two of silence to think about the question. Keep in mind, if silence doesn't bother you, it won't bother anyone else. After someone responds, affirm the response with a simple "thanks" or "good job." Then ask, "How about somebody else?" or "Would someone who hasn't shared like to add anything?" Be sensitive to new people or members who aren't ready to say, pray, or do anything. If you give them a safe setting, they will blossom over time.

7. Provide transitions between questions. When guiding the discussion, always read aloud the transitional paragraphs and the questions. Ask the group if anyone would like to read the paragraphs or Bible passages. Don't call on anyone, but ask for volunteers; then be patient until someone begins. Be sure to thank the people who read aloud.

8. Break up into small groups each week or a larger group won't stay. If your group has a lot of people, we strongly encourage you to have the group gather sometimes in discussion circles of three or four people during the **Encounter the Word, Engage Our Hearts, and Encourage Others** sections of the study. With a greater opportunity to talk in small circles, people will connect more with the study, apply more quickly what they're learning, and ultimately get more out of it. A small circle also encourages a quiet person to participate and tends to minimize the effect of a more dominant or vocal member. It can also help people feel more loved in your group.

   When you gather again at the end of the section, you can have one person summarize the highlights from each circle. Small circles are also helpful during prayer time. People who are not accustomed to praying aloud will feel more comfortable trying it with just two or three others.

   Also, prayer requests won't take as much time, so circles will have more time to actually pray. When you gather back with the whole group, you can have one person from each circle briefly update everyone on the prayer requests. People are more willing to break into small circles to pray if they know the whole group will hear all the prayer requests.

9. Rotate facilitators weekly. At the end of each meeting, ask the group who should lead the following week. Let the group help select your weekly facilitator. You may be perfectly capable of leading each time, but you will help others grow in their faith and gifts if you give them opportunities to

lead. You can use the Small Group Calendar (p. 200) to fill in the names of the different leaders for all the meetings if you prefer.

10. One final challenge (for new or first-time leaders): Before your first opportunity to lead, look up each of the five passages listed below. Read each one as a devotional exercise to help equip yourself with a shepherd's heart. Trust us on this one. If you do this, you will be more than ready to lead your first meeting.

Matthew 9:36
1 Peter 5:2–4
Psalm 23
Ezekiel 34:11–16
1 Thessalonians 2:7–8, 11–12

ACKNOWLEDGMENTS

I would like to acknowledge the talented, patient, flexible, and kind people who form the Bible Study Media team. It has been a pleasure to work with them throughout the various stages of the publishing process. I am especially grateful to Brooke and Charlie Holt who took on this study as a part of their mission to increase biblical literacy, and who worked so hard to usher it to completion. Many thanks to Chris Nott and Tommy Owen who captured the theological precepts so beautifully in the creative design of this book. I have the greatest appreciation for the attentive work of Joni Tapp and Karalee Reinke, who carefully edited my writing, making it much better than it was. For the talented and encouraging crew at Blueprint Film Company—Brooks Cruzen, Brian Frye, and Ray Kuglar—and the many behind-the-scenes players, I am very grateful. Thank you for bringing this project to fruition. God has had his hand on each stage of this project, and his imprint is evident.

I would like to thank the women of the Tuesday Women's Bible Study at the Church of the Good Shepherd in Corpus Christi, Texas, and all those who participated online in the initial version of this study in 2020. Your encouragement, wisdom, and insight were an inspiration to me and helped keep me on track.

I am blessed beyond measure by the faithful women who pray with me and for me. This book is only possibly by their prayers. I especially want to mention Lula Martin, Lorraine Volk, Betty Fuller, and Allison Schovee who have prayed faithfully for this project and for my teaching and writing ministry.

For the love, support, and encouragement of my family, especially my husband Milton, I am grateful beyond words! We do this together!

Finally, I give thanks to God, whose steady presence inspires and delights me. He strengthens me and accomplishes his purpose in me. No words are ever enough to capture the greatness of God. But I am thankful He calls me into the process. However inadequate are my words, Soli Deo gloria!

www.ingramcontent.com/pod-product-compliance
Lightning Source LLC
Chambersburg PA
CBHW040250090526
44586CB00040B/2622